Devil's Advocates

T0341934

DEVIL'S ADVOCATES is a series of books devoted to exploring the classics of horror cinema. Contributors to the series come from the fields of teaching, academia, journalism and fiction, but all have one thing in common: a passion for the horror film and a desire to share it with the widest possible audience.

'The admirable Devil's Advocates series is not only essential – and fun – reading for the serious horror fan but should be set texts on any genre course.'
Dr Ian Hunter, Reader in Film Studies, De Montfort University, Leicester

'Auteur Publishing's new Devil's Advocates critiques on individual titles... offer bracingly fresh perspectives from passionate writers. The series will perfectly complement the BFI archive volumes.' **Christopher Fowler,** *Independent on Sunday*

'Devil's Advocates has proven itself more than capable of producing impassioned, intelligent analyses of genre cinema... quickly becoming the go-to guys for intelligent, easily digestible film criticism.' *Horror Talk.com*

'Auteur Publishing continue the good work of giving serious critical attention to significant horror films.' *Black Static*

 DevilsAdvocatesbooks

 DevilsAdBooks

ALSO AVAILABLE IN THIS SERIES

FORTHCOMING

Devil's Advocates

The Curse of Frankenstein

Marcus K Harmes

Acknowledgments

My thanks are primarily due to John Atkinson, editor of this ongoing series, for advice and encouragement throughout the entire process from writing the proposal to completing the work. Dr Murray Leeder, a contributor to the Devil's Advocates series, also provided a number of helpful suggestions and I am grateful for these. Dr Matthew Jones of University College London answered a number of questions for me about 1950s cinema going. Dr Ian Hunter generously shared some forthcoming research with me. The interlibrary loans officers at the University of Southern Queensland have been uniformly helpful and successful in locating sources I have needed.

I dedicate this book to my mother and to Chloe and Suzette.

Bibliographic Note

All quotations from Mary Shelley's novel are taken from the 1985 edition by the Penguin Classics, edited by Maurice Hindle. Quotations from the 1957 film *The Curse of Frankenstein* are my own transcriptions.

First published in 2015 by
Auteur, 24 Hartwell Crescent, Leighton Buzzard LU7 1NP
www.auteur.co.uk
Copyright © Auteur 2015

Series design: Nikki Hamlett at Cassels Design
Set by Cassels Design www.casselsdesign.co.uk
Printed and bound by CPI Group (UK) Ltd, Croydon, CR0 4YY

British Library Cataloguing-in-Publication Data
A catalogue record for this book is available from the British Library

ISBN (paperback): 978-1-906733-85-8
ISBN (ebook): 978-0-9930717-0-6

CONTENTS

INTRODUCTION

A face like a car crash

The Curse of Frankenstein was a sensation on its release on 2 May 1957. Queues formed around blocks and it was a financial success for Hammer Film Productions, the company which made it. But it prompted dire predictions from film critics that it would debase civilisation. Certainly there was a great deal that was tacky about this film, at least by the standards of 1950s Britain. It was made in Kodak Eastman Color, a crude film processing method that made up for its cheapness by giving the director and cinematographer a range of startling and vivid hues, especially red. *The Curse of Frankenstein* revels in its redness, from liquids in chemical flasks to the glow of the batteries powered by the cross-rotational discs of the Wimshurst machine to a character's red silk dressing gown or the red berries in the forest near the Frankenstein chateau, and most horrifyingly of all, the creature's red eye after it has been shot in the face (Meikle, 2009: 43; Collins, 2012). Further tackiness was ensured by the decoration of cinema foyers with laboratory equipment, skeletons and a mannequin of the headless creature suspended in a tank, against which members of the cast and crew playfully posed at the premiere pretending to strangle each other (Meikle, 2009: 44). Posters for the film carried the tagline 'The Curse of Frankenstein will haunt you forever'. Another promised 'No one who saw it lived to describe it!' on a poster showing the star Peter Cushing toying with infernal apparatus and the monster looming over a screaming female in a negligee.

Critics wished it had never been made and hoped that the film, the company making it, and the popular demand for their wares, would all go away. But my entry point for analysing this film as a landmark work of major significance in film history is the way it defied these wishes. While the hyperbole of the poster that the film will haunt us forever is now just a quaint reminder of canny movie advertising, the tagline still has meaning. *The Curse of Frankenstein* remains, close to sixty years after its production, a visible and important cinematic commodity. It remains in print as a DVD release; it has been shown at commemorative film festivals; and it remains a source of topical (and mostly appreciative) discussion in online sites such as Rotten Tomatoes and the Internet Movie Database. If it has not exactly haunted us forever, it has continued to matter to ilm-makers, film historians, theorists, bloggers, critics and viewers, who have extensively discussed the movie, its makers and stars, and its impact and influence, including over more recent 'period horrors' such as Kenneth Branagh's *Mary Shelley's Frankenstein* (1994) to the adaptations of Anne Rice's vampire novels. The recent commercial revival of Hammer Film Productions and the box office success of the company's remake of *The Woman in Black* with Daniel Radcliffe in the starring role, has only served to again bring the Hammer name and its output of gothic cinema back into public consciousness. This gothic tradition has a starting point: *The Curse of Frankenstein*.

THE FILM IN HISTORY

The film is remembered in a number of ways and for a number of reasons. Exemplifying the theory that even bad publicity is good publicity, *Curse* is remembered as a box office sensation that didn't just make the careers of stars Peter Cushing and Christopher Lee, but established the name and fortunes of the film's production company, Hammer Film Productions. Hammer had been in business since the 1930s and in 1936 it brought fading horror star Bela Lugosi across to Britain to star in *Phantom Ship* (Miller, 1995: 43). The company fell into abeyance in World War Two but resumed production in the 1940s, overseen by Managing Director James Carreras and producers Anthony Hinds and Anthony Nelson-Keys. By 1951 the company had purchased Down Place, a Georgian country house in Berkshire that had been converted to house film studios (Miller, 1995: 45). Bray's facilities were small scale in comparison to other studios and the tightness and closeness of the working conditions came to define the work done there by a close knit team.

Particular team members stand out. Film historians generally note that it is the film that launched the international careers of actors Peter Cushing and Christopher Lee. Cushing played Baron Victor Frankenstein. He was 44 years old when *Curse* was released in 1957. He went on to star in dozens more horror and fantasy films, including playing Grand Moff Tarkin in 1977's *Star Wars*. Lee, now Sir Christopher Lee, is younger than Cushing (he was born in 1922). At the time of writing he is still going strong as the world's most prolific actor, including recent prominent roles in the *Star Wars* prequels as Count Dooku (an obvious nod to his role as Hammer's Count Dracula), in the *Lord of the Rings* films and *The Hobbit* as Saruman the White (more cinematic villainy deriving from Lee's Hammer work). He is the recipient of a British Film Institute fellowship, a mark of cultural respectability far removed from the period of *Curse*'s release when the film and its makers and stars gained overnight notoriety, especially Lee who was covered in horrifying makeup as the monster. Cushing and Lee became the 'unholy two' in the press, inextricably associated with each other and with the horror genre (Hutchinson, 1996: 85). In reality they only appeared in 22 films together, but their impact makes it seem much more.

Lee, Cushing and Hammer are names that are tightly associated with each other, but not as a trifecta, as there are four names at the heart of this movie, Cushing, Lee, Hammer, and then Terence Fisher (1904-1980), the film's director. Fisher had worked his way up the ranks from clapper boy to editor to director, including early Hammer science fiction genre efforts *Four Sided Triangle* (1953) and *Spaceways* (1953). Fisher's films before *Curse* were modest; they were certainly competent and even received the occasional positive review, but provide no meaningful prelude to the sudden spectacular success and critical condemnation of his first gothic horror.

THE STUDY

Success breeds success. Hammer's managing director James Carreras and his team of executives, producers and writers realised they had a hit and began making sequels and other gothic horrors. In quick succession they made more Frankenstein films, a series of Dracula films, and began to produce other monster films such as *The Mummy* (1959), *The Hound of the Baskervilles* (1959) and *Curse of the Werewolf* (1961). In the end, Hammer made seven Frankenstein films, almost as many Dracula films, and innumerable other genre efforts, including iterations of the Jekyll and Hyde and Phantom of the Opera stories, films based on the Jack the Ripper killings and others based on the gothic fiction of J Sheridan le Fanu. Hammer continued making horrors for nearly twenty years, ending with 1976's *To the Devil, A Daughter*, again with Christopher Lee pressed into service. Cushing kept playing Baron Frankenstein up until 1974's *Frankenstein and the Monster from Hell*.

This then is how *Curse of Frankenstein* is remembered, as the foundation of twenty years' worth of gothic horror and of the commercial and cinematic exploitation of public tastes for gore and violence. In a similar vein Hammer is remembered as opening a floodgate of domestic British and international gothic horror production that began at Bray but which was swiftly emulated as horror again became economically viable. In Britain film makers Milton Subotsky (who had actually contributed an early draft for *The Curse of Frankenstein*) founded Amicus and Tony Tenser founded Tigon, both companies committed to horror production. The small company Anglo-Amalgamated predated Hammer's gothic success, but also in the late 1950s moved into horror production following Hammer's example, making among others the vivid *Horrors of the Black Museum* (1959) and the early exploitation features *Peeping Tom* (1960, which attracted even worse press than *Curse of Frankenstein*) and *Circus of Horrors* (1960). The producer Monty Berman, a film maker almost as indefatigable as James Carreras, borrowed Hammer's script writer Jimmy Sangster to create period horrors including *Blood of the Vampire* (1958) and *Jack the Ripper* (1959) (Hamilton, 2013: 56-61). Both were period horrors and *Blood* was made in Eastman Color, although as a protagonist its star Vincent Ball was no match for Peter Cushing and the films lacked the energy that characterises Fisher's work.

The queues forming to see Hammer's early movies were noted by film makers elsewhere, such as Roger Corman who produced a cycle of lush gothic horrors for American International Pictures, a company that subsequently made a number of horror films in Britain. In Europe, film makers such as Luigi Carpentieri (often credited under anglicised pseudonyms to try to convey the impression they might be British film makers) launched gothic cinema onto continental audiences, including the ornate Baroque horrors starring the British actress Barbara Steele such as *The Terrible Secret of Dr Hichcock* (1962) and *Nightmare Castle* (1965).

But this trajectory can bury the original film under the influence of its own impact and what it spawned. Success once consolidated and repeated can obscure the novelty of the original. *Curse* can and has been buried; most comment and discussion tends to diminish the film by treating as merely a starting point, not as a creative output in its own right. I aim to recapture the impact of this novelty by looking at *Curse* not as the origin of a tradition that by 1976 had gone stale but as something fresh and new for audiences in 1957 and as a dramatically powerful hybrid adapted from contrasting sources. Assessments of *Curse* are often looking forwards, to the next twenty years, and view *Curse* as the forerunner of those twenty years of horror production. Again, this buries the film, encasing it as the forerunner of later achievements. If we move our position and start thinking about the film the other way – as in where it came from, not where it went in terms of its influence – we get a more singular impression of a film that is a landmark in its own right and as a transgressive adaptation that generated high levels of cultural interest.

My overall goal in this study is to assess *The Curse of Frankenstein* not as the harbinger of later horror films, but to consider instead the film's presumptive relationship to its literary and cinematic past and as an adaptation that is a powerful hybrid of literature and film. In particular I will show the film, or rather its creators, as omnivorous adapters and users, not just of Shelley's novel and not just of the renowned 1931 Universal *Frankenstein*. Rather the film appears in this study as a transgressive, textually complex adaptation, drawing on a diversity of resources. One way to think about this process of adaption is as triangulation: between the film, literary sources, and earlier film adaptations.[1] This process results in films with complex and often troubled reputations; they may not be as 'good' as an original, or faithful to the source or sources. But adaptations can also raise high levels of interest and they can be accessible. In 1956 Hammer's creative personnel turned to Shelley's novel to provide the basis of their film, and in doing so they were treading a well-worn path. But swirling around were yet more influences, from the dregs of poverty row horror and the Universal horror comedies, to the extremely limited indigenous British horrors from the pre-war period. *Curse* also shocked critics by placing the horrors in the recognisable settings of a Georgian drawing room and the surrounds of period drama and seems to be an unholy fusion of respectable heritage and disgusting horror.

Even the casting of Peter Cushing as Baron Victor Frankenstein contributed to this impact, as before starring in *Curse* Cushing was known primarily as a television actor in period costume productions, including playing Mr Darcy in a BBC adaptation of *Pride and Prejudice*. The study overall will pursue this film's production and impact as (in the eyes of almost all contemporary reviewers) as an offensive appropriation of earlier literary cinematic traditions. I read *Curse* not as a follow up to Hammer's science fiction successes, nor as a revival of a flagging horror industry, nor as the modest first step in the next twenty years of Hammer's horror production, all of which are the common takes on this film. Instead I locate it as a shocking example of a period or heritage film. The film places Baron Frankenstein, his fiancée, his servants and his monster in a *mise-en-scene* and setting adapted straight from glossy period dramas, but distorts them into ugliness and horror. On release critics trenchantly attacked the film, but hitherto studies of the film and its reception have not studied the way these reactions responded to the film and the way it was shocking because it was a transgressive adaptation.

In the chapters that follow I examine the creation and impact of *The Curse of Frankenstein* and how the film was not just a matter of bringing a well-known novel onto screen but in fact brought a range of different and even conflicting texts and storytelling traditions into dialogue with each other. I consider aspects of the film that have received limited attention or none at all. These include systematic analysis of the ways that it did but as importantly did not adapt from Shelley's novel, as well as full consideration of points that hitherto have only been footnotes to the history of the film, including the early comedy drafts and the importance of the Gainsborough melodramas in shaping its style and tone. In order, the chapters examine the production history and reception of the film, the way the Hammer company constantly adapted, then three case studies of adaption: from Shelley's novel, from poverty row and comedy horror, and from period drama. Thus in chapter two I consider in broader terms the adaptation of sources, before in chapter three considering the far from clear cut relationship between the novel and the film. In chapter four my focus moves to the traditions of horror film making prior to 1956, including the much maligned Universal horror comedy mashups of the 1940s and 1950s, films that are mostly disregarded by horror film historians but which I position as important aspects of *Curse*'s background. In chapter five I then consider a different film making tradition, the heritage and costume dramas of Gainsborough studios, assessing them as the breeding ground of the team that later coalesced at Hammer and as a key to understanding the transgressive nature of the film which critics found so shocking. But to start with in chapter one, I sketch in some introductory points about *Curse* including its narrative and what people thought of it in 1957. To reach that point we move attention to the confined, cramped but exciting environment of Bray Studios, where in 1956 a group of otherwise seeming staid and conservative film makers (almost all men) were embarking on a new project. This was something not before attempted in a British studio and it was, in the Britain of 1956, a frankly weird and unexpected thing to do: they were making *Frankenstein*.

FOOTNOTES

1.   The idea of triangulation is discussed by Hunter in his forthcoming chapter on Spielberg and adaptation in the *Blackwell Companion to Spielberg*, edited by Nigel Morris.

CHAPTER ONE: THE FILM AND ITS CRITICS

Reading reviews from 1957, it is clear that critics had not seen anything quite like *The Curse of Frankenstein* before. Their responses are valuable signifiers of what seemed so startling about it at the time of release. But before we move to those reviews and other critical reactions to the movie, a resumé of the plot is vital.

THE FILM

The trailer for *The Curse of Frankenstein* promised cinema audiences a thrilling slice of action involving a man who, so the dramatic voice over promises, 'revolted against nature' and who had 'experimented with the Devil and was forever cursed'. The trailer showed scenes of a bandaged figure lying in the midst of antiquated (by the standards of the 1950s) laboratory equipment, and of a well-dressed man informing an equally dapper companion that 'we've discovered the source of life itself'. The monster itself was only very briefly glimpsed in the trailer, ensuring that audiences would have to buy tickets to see the film in order to witness the full horror.

The action in *The Curse of Frankenstein* is told in a flashback by a series of reminiscences by Baron Frankenstein, waiting in a condemned cell to be guillotined, to a priest brought to hear his confession. His story begins shortly after the death and burial of his mother the old Baroness Frankenstein, who has outlived her husband, the old Baron, and leaves behind her son. The son, (played by Melvyn Hayes) is still a teenager and is a brash and precious boy, barely capable of even the most basic civilities to the members of his family gathered for the funeral. He has engaged a tutor, Paul Krempe (Robert Urquart) to instruct him in anatomy and the natural sciences. Krempe remains the Baron's tutor as he grows to adulthood and the adult Victor Frankenstein (now played by Peter Cushing) and his tutor have been working of experiments intended to restore life to dead tissue. They have success in reviving a dead puppy.

However Krempe is perturbed by where Frankenstein wishes to take these experimental insights. Krempe had assumed that their work in suspending and restoring life could be used to improve surgical techniques and intends that they should present a paper at a scientific academy. The Baron has other ideas: he intends to construct and bring life to a human body. He tells Krempe that 'It's no longer sufficient to being the dead back to life. We must create from the beginning. We must build up our own creature.' He commences a series of robberies from gibbets, tombs and charnel houses to assemble the parts he needs to create a body. These include the corpse of a gibbeted criminal, hands from a master sculptor and eyes from a charnel house. Stitched together, suspended in an eerie liquid and chemical concoction in a tank, and blasted with electricity during a storm, the creature comes to life.

The creature is 'born' in the amniotic fluid

By this point Frankenstein and Krempe have parted company, Krempe concerned not only by his former pupil's ambition to play god and create a living man, but also by the increasingly illegal methods Frankenstein was employing to get body parts. This lawlessness culminated in the Baron's quest for a brain. Determined to have a brain of fine intellect and life experience in his creation, Frankenstein murders an eminent scientist, Professor Bernstein (Paul Hardtmuth), steals the brain from the crypt and implants it in the creature. While all the scientific work has been taking place, the Baron has become engaged, but keeps his laboratory locked and his work that takes him to the charnel house and cemetery separate from the civilised life he leads with his fiancée, Elizabeth (Hazel Court). He is also keeping secret that he has been having an affair with his servant Justine (Valerie Gaunt), who is now pregnant.

This narrative occupies the first half of the film. A turning point is reached when the creature awakes prematurely due to a blast of lightning activating the electrical equipment in the laboratory. The director Terence Fisher vividly captures the shock of its birth and first movement. Victor leaves the laboratory to fetch help but the amniotic fluid in the tank begins to drain away, visually suggesting the sand in an eggtimer running out as genesis approaches. Hearing noises, Frankenstein returns to the lab, pushes open the door and the creature turns to face him. Fisher uses a jarring and unnervingly jagged zoom from an over cranked camera to the creature's face as it turns and the bandages fall away from its face, ramming home the shock that Frankenstein feels as the camera tracks through the door and into the room (Collins, 2012). The Baron and the audience simultaneously see a pasty white face with a milky dead eye, horrific scarring and a violent leer. The creature is hideous when it was to have been handsome, mute when it should have been eloquent, and most of all violent when it should have been cultivated, a fact shown when it promptly attempts to strangle the Baron.

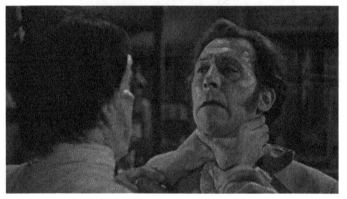

From the outset the creator has a difficult relationship with his creation

Thereafter the film moves briskly as the creature escapes, is hunted and is shot in the eye by Krempe. Buried in the forest, the creature is retrieved by Frankenstein and taken to the laboratory. It is revived by the Baron but is brain damaged and murderous. It has already killed a blind beggar and his grandchild and now kills Justine, the Baron's pregnant servant. Having pursued Frankenstein's fiancée to the rooftop of their chateau, the creature is set on fire by the Baron and shot, falling down into a vat of acid that dissolves its body. The creature's disappearance in the acid leaves no other suspects for the death of Justine except Frankenstein, and the film's action resolves back to the cell, with the Baron telling his story to the priest. It ends on this irony of the Baron being led to the guillotine for a crime he only indirectly committed, by virtue of having made the creature. As a bell tolls, the camera remains focussed on the guillotine blade and the closing credits roll.

The fate awaiting the Baron

ITS CREATION: THE STUDIO

Why make a Frankenstein picture in 1950s Britain? The place to look for the answer to this question is Bray Studios in Buckinghamshire, a few kilometres outside London. Bray Studios were set around Down Place, an elegant white country house set in very extensive grounds, and had been a film studio since the 1930s. By the 1950s it belonged to Hammer Film Productions. The interiors of the Baron's house and laboratory were filmed inside Down Place, and the exterior scenes, including Cushing scaling a gibbet to cut down the corpse and the creature killing the beggar and his grandson and then being hunted and shot, were filmed nearby in Black Park in Berkshire.

A core body of executives and creative personnel set upon an adaptation of Shelley's novel, which began principal photography on 16 November 1956 and wrapped on 24

December the same year. The working atmosphere at Bray Studios has been so well documented and described that this atmosphere remains palpable nearly 60 years later, especially the sense that came to dawn on cast and crew that they were working on something special. At Bray a close-knit team of technicians, some of whom had worked together earlier at the equally close-knit Gainsborough studios, were joined by a small repertory of actors to make this film. Their work would have been a novelty to many of them. It was in colour, it was pushing the envelope to the absolute limit in terms of the level of violence and sexuality that the British Board of Film Classification would allow, and above all, it was a horror film.

Despised by critics, prohibited by censors and local authorities and shunned by studios, there had only been a handful of horrors in Britain before now. A tiny number of silent British films had contained elements of horror (Brown, 2013). A few more horror films were made following the introduction of sound, including 1933's *The Ghoul*, 1936's *The Man Who Changed His Mind*, 1939's *Dark Eyes of London* and 1945's *Dead of Night*. For *Dark Eyes of London*, one of Hollywood's fading horror stars Bela Lugosi had come to England to make the film. The first two starred Boris Karloff, an actor and horror star who was British but whose career and therefore his major horror appearances were made in Hollywood productions. But now at Bray Studios, horror had 'come home'. Hollywood horrors had been contingent on British source novels, but British film makers themselves had not regarded this literary heritage as suitable source material for movies.

Nothing in their early output suggests that the Hammer name would become a byword for gothic horror or the company a major commercial success, and the films prior to 1957 were an eclectic bunch of movies from detective stories to attempts at noir to science fiction and melodrama. None of them was particularly distinguished or important and were mostly modest B features, just as the Hammer films of the 1930s had been 'quota quickies' made to satisfy government demand for native British films. This circumstance changed when the studio achieved commercial success with science fiction features *The Quatermass Xperiment*, *Quatermass 2*, and *X the Unknown*, during the mid-1950s. The first two of these were adaptations of successful BBC science fiction serials written by Nigel Kneale that Hammer made into popular films (popular that is with everyone except Kneale, who hated what Hammer did to his work) and *X the*

Unknown was a science fiction thriller by Jimmy Sangster, who also wrote the script for *Curse*.

Then in 1957 *Curse* film performed impressively at the British and American box office and recouped its production costs more than 70 times over (Hearn, 2011: 15) as well as performing strongly in both the West End and in regional theatres (Meikle, 2009: 41). The box office returns made Hammer's executives realise they had a winning pattern on their hands, and a sequel, *Revenge of Frankenstein*, and another gothic horror, *Dracula* (both released in 1958) were soon in production, the former using Cushing again as the Baron and the latter reuniting Cushing and Lee (with Cushing as Van Helsing and Lee as the Count), all directed by Terence Fisher.

ITS CREATION: THE DIRECTOR

Terence Fisher died in 1980 in relative obscurity; few newspapers carried obituaries, either recounting his life or, more significantly, attempting to locate the director and his work in any meaningful frame of reference that might make sense of his career and impact. Before his death he had received academic attention in only one major text, David Pirie's landmark work *Heritage of Horror* (1973). But since Fisher's death, and more particularly in the last twenty years, he has received extensive attention from film historians and theorists, including biographies by Wheeler Winston Dixon and Peter Hutchings, study of the religious themes in his works by Paul Leggett, as well as descriptions, evaluations and accounts of his career and life in general studies of Hammer by Meikle and Johnson and del Vecchio, in Pirie's pioneering academic study of British horror cinema, and in works in British directors and the British film industry (Hutchings 2001; Leggett, 2002).

The Curse of Frankenstein receives attention in all these works. In the most positive assessments, Fisher is considered an auteur, a director with a unique creative vision which imbues his oeuvre with particular and consistent artistic qualities. At the other end of the spectrum Fisher is written off as a hack and a plodder who made derivative and uninteresting films. Somewhere in the middle we can try to locate a vision of Fisher who was a late-comer to the film industry in general and to directing in particular (he was a merchant seamen before working in the film industry and once described himself as the 'oldest clapper boy in the business'). He was in the right place at the right time when Hammer's executives decided to make a gothic horror in 1956 and who was put in charge of a team of industry professionals with years of experience. Viewing the films that Fisher directed from *Colonel Bogey* in 1947 to *Frankenstein and the Monster from Hell* in 1972 (released 1974) reinforces his competence and the professional standard of his work. By the time the cameras started rolling at Bray in 1956 Fisher was ready to apply what he had learnt in another studio, Gainsborough.

ITS CREATION: THE TEAM

By the mid-1950s a team was working at Hammer under the adroit commercial leadership of the managing director James Carreras, including writer Jimmy Sangster, cinematographer Jack Asher, set designer Bernard Robinson, make-up artist Philip Leakey, composer James Bernard, producers Anthony Nelson Keys and Anthony Hinds, and Fisher.

Right from the start the remarkably vigorous quality of the team's work was obvious; the first scene filmed was the Baron cutting down the hanged robber from the gibbet and Cushing performed the dangerous climb to the top of the gibbet prop himself. The same level of energy carries through the entire production. A palpable sense of excitement among the actors and technicians squeezed into the small studio spaces at Bray still registers, reaching out to us across the decades. The team making *Curse* was harmonious and the cramped working conditions at Bray were homely compared to the vastness of Pinewood, Borehamwood, Ellstree or Shepperton. The close-knit arrangement was encouraged further by the crew being bussed into Bray and home again each day. Black and white photos of the behind the scenes action convey the cosiness of the working environment. In one remarkable image, Lee in his monster make up and with fake blood down his face is getting a cup of tea from that most British of things, the tea lady with her trolley. The crew had worked together before and would do so again; Sangster and Fisher had worked at Hammer on a number of B features before collaborating on *Curse*. According to the autobiography of leading man Christopher Lee, there was a vibrant atmosphere on the set, and the original five-week period that the company allocated for filming was extended to six when the managing director realised 'that we were onto something and the ship mustn't be spoilt for a ha'p'orth of tar' (Lee 1997: 251). Production schedules and budgets had to be extended, but the early rushes convinced executives to make the effort (Dixon, 1991: 226).

The team behind the cameras was close-knit one; so too was the team acting out the drama in front of the cameras. Cushing was quite a catch for Hammer, after successes he scored on television playing Winston Smith in the BBC's *1984* (a dramatisation savaged by appalled critics but which was a major hit for the BBC in terms of audience and which won Cushing a BAFTA), as well as Mr Darcy in an adaptation of *Pride and Prejudice* in 1952. Christopher Lee's date with destiny, and the beginning of his career in horror cinema that has placed him in the *Guinness Book of Records* as the world's most prolific actor, came about because he was tall enough to be the monster. It could just as easily have been Bernard Bresslaw playing the monster, but Bresslaw was soon to be busy with another long-running British cinematic success, the *Carry On* films. The rest of the cast were reliable theatre and film performers. Hazel Court, playing the Baron's fiancée Elizabeth, had made a name for herself in period drama and science fiction films, including the unforgettable 1954 thriller *Devil Girl from Mars*. The Scottish actor Robert Urquhart came into Hammer's orbit from wartime-set dramas such as *Yangtse Incident* (1957), and after *Curse* went right back to that sort of film, appearing as reliable supporting player in *Dunkirk* (1958), *55 Days in Peking* (1963) and other worthy historical dramas. Valerie Gaunt stepped out from humdrum police drama *Dixon of Dock Green* to play the vampish maid Justine. Such is the small-scale, claustrophobic inner world that Fisher creates, that this quintet of performers Lee, Cushing, Urquhart, Court and Gaunt, account for virtually the entire cast. There are a handful of subsidiary roles (the priest, the Professor, the blind old man, the comedy relief drunk Burgomaster and his censorious wife) but mostly the film plays out its length just with focus on these four people and the monster.

FILMING AND BUDGET

One change in particular registers on the screen from Hammer's successful science fiction films *X the Unknown* and the *Quatermass* as well as the earlier celebrated adaptation of Shelley's novel directed by James Whale for Universal Pictures in 1931:

The Curse of Frankenstein is in colour. Not only is it in colour, it is made and processed in Eastman Color, which shows up in lurid glory the dark red. As Arthur Marwick points out, in 1957 the vast majority of British films were still being made in black and white, meaning the colour of the horrors on the screen stood out strongly (1991: 74).

Eastman Color is a relatively cheap film processing method, and it is one the many cheap aspects of the film. £64,000 is not a great deal to spend on a film, even by the standards of 1956. In some ways this budgetary restraint shows on screen, but in others it is remarkably well hidden. It shows in that except for the framing scenes in the Baron's jail cell and the brief chase sequence filmed in Black Park, the action almost never leaves the Baron's chateau and its upstairs laboratory. The contrast with contemporary horror films made at larger studios is instructive; 1959's *The Flesh and the Fiends* was made at Shepperton and is an expansive film, showcasing large sets and street scenes of nineteenth-century Edinburgh. Sangster's screenplay for *Curse* drastically condenses Shelley's novel, removing not only characters but the immense transcontinental pursuit of the Creature by Frankenstein that ends on the Arctic. Frankenstein's visits to London, Scotland and his inadvertent trip to Ireland (when he is washed up on the shore after floating adrift from a Scottish island) are all missing. So too are the periods of study Frankenstein enjoys in Ingolstadt. Sangster's narrative rarely moves beyond the dual worlds the Baron inhabits, the respectable world of the downstairs which he shares with his fiancée and with polite society, and the upstairs world of bio-mechanical science filled with acid and infernal machinery.

The limited budget shows in other ways. The cast is small and there are almost no extras. There is certainly no torch wielding mob familiar from other adaptations of the story. Many of Shelley's original characters are lost, from Frankenstein's father, brothers (including his ill-fated younger brother who is murdered by the monster) and friends, the professors at Ingolstadt, the three De Laceys who live in the cottage and who have a terrifying encounter with the creature, the Irish magistrate who exonerates Frankenstein of a murder charge, and above all Captain Walton, the intrepid seafarer who encounters both Frankenstein and his creature in the Arctic ice and nurses the dying scientist on board his ship. The sets are also small, although scenic designer Bernard Robinson, cinematographer Jack Asher and director Terence Fisher make the most of the angles afforded by the cramped but interesting interiors at Bray.

But in other ways the budget's limits are extremely well hidden, not just in the deceptively spacious scenes captured by Fisher's camera. Even by 1956 British cinema had a long tradition of period or costume drama, a point I'll return to later. On screen, this experience shows in the immaculate costume and scenographic design. None of this looks especially authentic or accurate, and what is meant to be Switzerland in 1818 looks like England from the previous century. However what is missing in terms of strict historical accuracy is made up for in the well-appointed and detailed sets. In Baron Frankenstein's downstairs and respectable world, he and his fiancée entertain guests in their drawing room. The Baron drinks brandy, smokes cigars, wears a velvet smoking jacket and their meals are lavish affairs. Upstairs the laboratory, while an ugly and technological space in contrast to the gracious domestic comforts downstairs, is also well-appointed. The talented and resourceful Bernard Robinson decorated the set with genuine antique laboratory equipment (Miller, 1995: 49). He also included small but telling details; a skull sits on a side desk, while red fire buckets with water hang on the walls, prefiguring the fiery climax. A large Wimshurst machine that activates glowing red lights is a centrepiece and used to reanimate the creature, as its dual wheels spin and (real and ridiculously dangerous) electrical charge builds up and crackles. To listen for a heartbeat the Baron used an authentic wooden tubular Pinard stethoscope. Overall Hammer's team managed to disguise their budgetary limitations to a remarkable degree in their sturdy and even lush evocation of period interiors.

A vintage Pinard stethoscope lets the Baron hear a heartbeat

ITS RECEPTION: PART ONE

Regardless of how happy the cast and crew were making the film or how good it looked, these points did not register with the critics in both Britain and America who saw the film on release, although the critical commentary from the British critics was the more trenchant. People could first see the film when it opened at the London Pavilion on 2 May, 1957. Readers of the *Sunday Times* were informed by film critic Dilys Powell that she was unable 'to defend the cinema against the charge it debases'. Similar terminology appeared in the *Tribune*: the film was 'depressing and degrading for anyone who loves the cinema'. One of the best known reviews oft-quoted in writings about Hammer was Derek Hill's in *Sight and Sound* which opined the film presented details 'immediately reminiscent of concentration camp atrocities' (cited in Cooper, 2011: 31). Executive producer Anthony Hinds was quoted in *The Times* as being 'undismayed by being called (to quote his own words) "a monster, a ghoul who exploits the basest, most degraded tastes in human nature for personal profit".' (cited in Fox, 2013). But reviewers blamed the director, not the producer. In *The Daily Worker* the critic R.D. Smith singled out Terence Fisher as responsible for 'splattering the screen with blood, gory sacking, human eyeballs torn from their sockets, amputated limbs' (cited in Miller, 1995: 67). Not all reviewers took the film so seriously and Hutchings points to a body of reviews that lightly mocked, such as the *Financial Times*'s opinion that horror films were eccentric light entertainment (Hutchings 2004: 85). In fact not all reviews were negative and some reviewers actually enjoyed the film; some were even frightened (Dixon, 1991: 234).

Viewers of much more recent horror films from *The Loved Ones* (2009) to the examples of the burgeoning 'torture porn' genre such as *Saw* or *Hostel* would find little horrific in Fisher's very stately film. Fisher keeps almost all the gore off screen, just below the edge of the visible shot. A great deal of the violence is only implied as well. Three murders are committed in the course of the film; the old blind peasant, his grandson and the maid Justine are all killed by the creature. Viewers do not see any of these. We hear Justine scream as the monster advances; the boy's death is even more obliquely suggested. He wanders off screen in the general direction of the monster, and later Fisher's camera pans down to the ground to show his satchel trampled into the dirt. It is sixteen minutes into the running time before Fisher shows anything at all gory, and this is the gibbet. Once the hanged criminal's corpse is back in the laboratory there is a tantalising glimpse of the decomposing face, but Fisher's camera quickly tracks up and the sight is gone. Fisher allows only the briefest glimpse of a scalpel before cutting back to the master shot (Dixon, 1991: 244). We hear a splash as the Baron drops the head in the acid bath, but the camera is trained on Cushing's face and again we see nothing. Fisher's adroit use of suggestion rather than display defines the film. At about 30 minutes in, the Baron invites Krempe to view his work, but the audience is excluded. Krempe recoils in horror from what is hidden behind a cloth, but the audience is left to guess. The most striking suggestiveness comes when Frankenstein buys the eyeballs from the charnel house. Fisher allows the viewer a very brief glimpse of the eyeballs in a container but then cuts immediately to a close-up of Frankenstein examining the eyeballs (which are out of shot) back in the laboratory. The Baron is holding up a magnifying glass which grossly distorts and expands his own eye. Without having to show the disembodied eyeballs, Fisher has compellingly indicated that the whole sequence is about eyes.[2] It is more than half way through the running length that Fisher shows anything really nasty, and that is the monster's face. Fisher in fact took pains to ingeniously suggest rather than show. When the creature is shot in the eye, there is a very brief glimpse of blood, but more telling of the physical and cerebral turmoil is the effect of the autumnal leaves suddenly swirling and blowing around the creature, visually suggesting the dreadful damage the bullet is doing inside the creature's brain. These impressions are conveyed by suggestion, not by explicitness. But what little gore there was, it was still too much for the critics in 1957.

Why did they hate it so much? Viewing the film in the twenty-first century it is hard to wonder what all the fuss was about. Not only has the horror genre moved into the torture porn realm, it has reached this point after earlier phases of development from the slasher horror, urban horror and sexploitation films such as the exceptionally controversial I Spit on your Grave (1978), Pete Walker's mid-1970s output and the 1970s sub genres such the 'women in prison' films and nunsploitation. We also view Fisher's film in the twenty-first century after the 'video nasties' moral panic of the early 1980s, which resulted in a large number of films being banned in Britain including Mother's Day (1980) and The Burning (1981) as well as a host of Italian horrors (Kendrick, 2004: 162). All of these films make the implied and mostly off-screen surgical procedures in Curse of Frankenstein seem tame. As well, many developments in the horror genre have tended to eschew the period settings of Hammer, preferring contemporary and often urban settings, from Phoenix, Arizona in *Psycho*, to Haddonfield, Illinois in *Halloween*. The period setting of *Curse* can seem in contrast remote and the pace sedate.

But these later genres and trends all come in the wake of *Curse of Frankenstein*. Critics seeing it in 1957 were part of a film culture that privileged particular themes and outputs. A comment in the newspaper the *Evening Advertiser* from that year is revealing, asking rhetorically 'Where would British films be without the Royal Navy?' (Carney, 2013: 136). A survey of films released in 1957 and in the years immediately before helps put the venom of the critics into context and makes sense of the *Evening Advertiser*'s observation. British audiences and critics were used to a steady diet of worthy films such as 1957's *Yangtse Incident* (the one commented on by the reviewer in the *Evening Advertiser*), one of many 'stiff upper lip' war dramas that proliferated on screen. Also in 1957 there came *Ill Met by Moonlight* and the highly regarded *The Bridge on the River Kwai*. Other popular cinematic types of the time were jolly comedies (*Blue Murder at St Trinian's* and *Doctor at Large* also came out in 1957) and respectable period dramas such as *The Barretts of Wimpole Street*. These trends continued, suggesting the extent to which at its premiere in 1957 *The Curse of Frankenstein* must have seemed freakishly bizarre. The next year the *Carry On* series of amiable sex comedy films began with *Carry On Sergeant*, and in 1959 box office records were broken by *Carry On Nurse* (Ross, 2005: 26).

There were occasional horror films as well. *Night of the Demon*, a British-made film with an American star (Dana Andrews) and director (Jacques Tourneur), and now a cult favourite, appeared in 1957. But this film was in black and white, and was mostly subtle compared to what must have been the brightly coloured shocks of Frankenstein's laboratory. As we shall see later in this discussion, *Curse of Frankenstein* was preceded by a sporadic but clearly apparent tradition of horror cinema, even from such unlikely sources as Abbott and Costello. In 1957, in Britain, however, the film burst onto screen amidst a large number of black and white, respectable, patriotic and very harmless British films. One film historian calls the 1950s output of the British film industry 'constipated' (Ashworth, 1996: 301). The term admirably sums up the moral safeness of films of the period, especially those made by the dominant Rank Organisation headed by the teetotal Methodist Lord J. Arthur Rank.

Some reviewers actively hoped to discourage people – especially young people – from going to see *The Curse of Frankenstein*. Dire warnings were all ignored as the film performed brisk business in Britain, the US and then in Europe as well. For an outlay of £64,000, or $270,000, the film made between $7-8 million. Among those seeing the film was John Carpenter. As an adult, Carpenter became a film director, producer, editor and musician. As a child he was captivated by Hammer's film and its tagline '*The Curse of Frankenstein* will haunt you forever!' Carpenter has since asserted the seminal influence of Fisher over horror cinema, not only in prompting outpourings of criticism against the genre but in the way Fisher carefully orchestrated his 'sequences of blood and mayhem' (Carpenter in Dixon, 1991: xi). In the years and decades since the film's release, other directors from Tim Burton to Martin Scorsese have cited seeing Fisher's films as a seminal childhood experience. Burton's 1999 (and British-made) horror *Sleepy Hollow* not only included a cameo from Christopher Lee in a very Hammer-style role as a judge but was also assessed by many critics as a clear homage to Hammer's style (Salisbury, 1999). Twenty years' after *Curse* came out George Lucas drew much of the cast for *Star Wars* from the ranks of Hammer alumnus, most prominently Peter Cushing.

This box office success came both despite and because of the film's X certificate from the British Board of Film Censorship (BBFC). The peculiar spelling of Hammer's earlier feature *The Quatermass Xperiment*, not to mention their next science fiction feature's title *X the Unknown* were entirely unsubtle references to the fact their films were deemed horrifying enough to warrant an X certificate, restricting an audience to people 16 years and over.

At least before Hammer came to boast in their titles about getting them, an X certificate (which had been issued since 1951) was normally something avoided at all cost, although the idea that a restrictive certificate would boost business was not new as the producers of *Dark Eyes of London* in 1939 had requested an H (for 'Horror') certificate for their film (Johnson, 1997: 159). The major cinema chains often declined to show X features and they were generally a mark of a disreputable product (Hutchings, 2003: 29). The X certificate existed simply because the BBFC needed something to label films deemed too frightening, sickening or generally unpalatable that they should only be seen by an age restricted audience. For any other film executive, an X certificate would have been a disaster, but James Carreras didn't bat an eyelid and turned a mark of critical opprobrium into a marketing ploy. Carreras, was in no doubt that getting an X certificate meant that his films were instantly branded as disreputable. Indeed he was apprehensive when some years after *Curse*'s release the British Film Institute suggested organising a special screening of Hammer's films, saying that Hammer's success lay in *not* being respectable.[3]

Thus the film that critics attacked in such alarmist tones on its release in 1957 came out with an X certificate from the BBCF, meaning that its audience was age restricted and it came with a reputation preceding it, as a work deemed horrifying by Britain's censors. We should not overlook the implication of its certificate when reading these reviews. Having an X certificate meant that *Curse* was in its own way cursed. Critics were primed to see in it degenerate film making. But, and this is a big 'but', the X certificate did not carry through on its normal implications. As I said, often major cinema chains would decline to show X features and this level of classification could restrict not only audiences but profitability. This was not the case with *Curse*. It pushed past these restrictions and gained an audience.

ITS RECEPTION - EXCURSUS: *PEEPING TOM*

A school of thought suggests that any publicity is good publicity but can we tie that point in to the reception of *The Curse of Frankenstein*? While the producer Anthony Hinds was happy to tell *The Times* that he didn't care if people thought he was a ghoul, not all of the production team were so relaxed. In an interview conducted in the 1970s and thus many years after the film's release, Terence Fisher recalled how upset he had been by the vitriol directed at his film and at him. This after all was a quiet, respectably married Christian man who was appalled by the scene in *The Exorcist* of the small girl playing Regan masturbating (Nicholson). While he could exploit mild doses of sex and violence, Fisher was far from being the depraved pervert reviewers suggested he was and has even been derided for his conventionality (Hutchings, 2001: 13; Harmes, 2014: 102).

There is more to being thin-skinned here: Fisher was right to be worried as the publicity which horror films generated could end careers. It is worthwhile moving forward just three years to 1960 where we find uncannily similar points of view being made against a horror film by the same set of critics, including the dangerously misguided Dilys Powell. The film is Michael Powell's 1960 psychological horror *Peeping Tom*, about a humble film crew's focus-puller who murders women and voyeuristically watches film he has shot of their death throes. Powell was, prior to 1960, an acclaimed film maker, responsible (in collaboration with Emeric Pressburger) for scores of films including *A Canterbury Tale* (1944), *Black Narcissus* (1947) and *The Red Shoes* (1948). These films won positive notices and they also won awards. *Peeping Tom* meanwhile was critically savaged. Once more Dilys Powell was shocked by the depths to which British cinema had sunk with this 'essentially vicious' movie. In the *Observer* newspaper C.A. Lejeune (who had walked out of the pre-screening) reported that 'It's a long time since a film disgusted me as much as Peeping Tom' (cited in Gritten, 2010). Lejeune had earlier informed the *Observer*'s readership that *Curse of Frankenstein* was 'among the half-dozen most repulsive films I have encountered' (cited in Miller, 1995: 67). Of *Peeping Tom* other critics asked 'why, oh why…?' in dramatic despair (Patterson, 2010).

The comments made against *Peeping Tom* provide important context and scope for the reviews of *The Curse of Frankenstein*. Clearly few horror film makers were likely to escape critical censure. But while almost every history of the Hammer studio, biography of Terence Fisher, and review of *Curse* has quoted the same highly critical reviews none, as far as I can judge, have reflected on the important distinction in the otherwise identical critical reception of *Curse* and *Peeping Tom*. The reviews killed off Michael Powell's career, indicating that in some instances bad publicity is just bad publicity, whereas *Curse* was a career-making film for Fisher, bad reviews and all. After *Peeping Tom* Powell became an outcast, going from being a critically lauded and prolific director to a man whose career ground to almost a halt and who made few other films until he died in 1990 (Gritten, 2010). To put it in perspective it would be as if a critical savaging had destroyed the career of Sir David Lean or Sir Carol Reed. Fisher by contrast, while personally upset by the bad reviews, weathered the storm. *Curse*, critical savaging or not, made Fisher's career. Powell was a highly regarded award winning director; Fisher was a non-entity with much less to lose but a lot to gain. Following his first gothic horror, Fisher embarked on an astonishingly prolific horror career making another 23 films between 1957 and 1972, most for Hammer. *Curse* also defined him: the self-described 'journeyman director' who had done anything and everything from science fiction to whimsical comedy developed from one film a coherence in his later output that has enabled critics and biographers to seriously claim *auteur* status for him.

The parallels are neat but the contrast is striking. There are important explanations for the varied fortunes of two horror directors who films had such a similar reception. Fisher was working for a company who didn't care about critical savaging and actively courted it. James Carreras could turn a bad review into a marketing opportunity in a way few other British film executives could have managed. Fisher also had a studio infrastructure to back him up. After success with *Curse*, Hammer was not going to let him go, whereas Powell had so such repertory security to back him up. He was essentially on his own to face the negative reactions.

While almost all accounts and histories of Hammer have quoted these bad reviews, few seem to have gone further and thought in more sustained terms about what they may have signified and why Hammer's film survived a critical mauling when others did not. Having moved forward to 1960, moving backwards to the 1940s further illuminates this same point. The negative not to say hysterical, reviews against *Peeping Tom* had been prefigured by the reactions (often by the same critics) to *Curse* three years earlier; but in turn the reviews of *Curse* had been prefigured by the comments made about another instance of mass film culture, the Gainsborough melodramas. The Gainsborough costume dramas (some of them made by Fisher working with crew including Jack Asher and Anthony Nelson-Keys) were trenchantly attacked. One critic found a Gainsborough film *The Wicked Lady* (1945) nauseating (cited in Cook, 1996b: 55). To critics they seemed to be in the worst possible taste. Gainsborough executives were unperturbed and one of them, R.J. Minney, unapologetically argued that 'the commodity must be what the public wants' (cited in Harper, 1994: 120). Like Carreras, executives at Gainsborough were prepared to weather the storm, confident that they had a commodity that audiences wanted and the films were generally box office successes (Cook, 1996b: 52; Petrie, 1997: 119). They also had a developing critical mass of product, Gainsborough with their costume cycle and Hammer with their gothic horrors. *Peeping Tom* was a one-off, not only because it ended Powell's career but it had at any rate always been intended as a stand-alone. The film that Fisher was purveying was of a type with a long-standing and entrenched genre of costume drama.

ITS RECEPTION: PART TWO

Reactions to *Curse* have over the decades become more measured but in some ways things have not improved in terms of *Curse*'s reputation. *Curse* and then Hammer's *Dracula*, released the next year, are the foundation of the company's gothic output. They are both adaptations of major gothic novels and both spawned a long series of sequels. They were both also the results of the same creative stable, and actors from *Curse* including Cushing, Lee and Valerie Gaunt were all redeployed in *Dracula*, as well as having the same team including Fisher, Sangster, Asher, Hinds, Nelson Keys, Phil Leakey on makeup and James Bernard composing the score, all working behind the scenes for James Carreras. But a range of critical assessments almost always consign *Curse* to the lesser place, judging *Curse* as an experiment but *Dracula* as the consolidation and success. Peter Hutching's judgment is in many ways typical of these assessments. Thus he believes that *Curse* is less cinematically adroit, its camera work and design less confident, James Bernard's music is less impressive, the budget smaller than for *Dracula* (Hutchings, 2003: 36). The opening scenes seem 'tentative' in contrast to the opening of *Dracula* which is 'brasher, louder, bolder, innovative, more confident, more cinematic' (Hutchings, 2003: 37). In short, critical assessments such as these look at *Curse* strictly in terms of hindsight, as a modest beginning to the bigger and better films that followed and then to the less impressive films that Hammer kept churning out past their due by date.

These are by no means unique observations, but can have some correctives. In some measure there is truth in some of these points. Having experienced success with *Curse of Frankenstein*, Hammer's executives wanted more of the same. Confident they seemed to have a property – gothic horror – that audiences wanted they were also prepared to splash a bit more cash at the next film, *Dracula*. But these modern critical assessments have a deleterious effect on *Curse*'s reputation as much as the critical mauling of the 1950s had. They obscure what made *Curse* so offensive but also so startling in the way it adapted from earlier texts. Locating *Curse* as a modest first effort can push into the background why it shocked and therefore why it also mattered. In the next chapter I turn to the nature of adaptation, with the Hammer company in general and particularly with *The Curse of Frankenstein*.

FOOTNOTES

2.   The image of the magnifying glass held up to the eye became a trademark look for Cushing and was taken to ludicrous extremes in the 1984 spoof movie *Top Secret*, when Cushing's character lowers the magnifying glass to reveal a massively oversized eye behind it.

3.   The same fear of respectability did not preclude him from accepting a knighthood in 1970.

CHAPTER TWO: ADAPTING AND TRANSGRESSING

For a movie about a creature stitched together from an aggregation of body parts, it is apposite to think of the film itself as based on the joining together of different influences. As the credits say, it is an adaptation of Mary Shelley's 1818 novel *Frankenstein, or the Modern Prometheus*. While the title may have been a shorthand reference to an entire story-telling tradition and the controversy that accompanied it, the resultant film is best considered a 'transgressive adaptation', where the source selected for adaptation is ultimately a foundation for later deviation away from the original. Although most of the reviews on its release were critical, in particular attacking Fisher and his film for being degrading and violent, one positive review in *Punch* thought the film was a 'conscientious version of the novel' (cited in Meikle, 2009: 43). In its own way this comment is as strange and misplaced as the trenchant attacks that thought going to see *The Curse of Frankenstein* would be a debasing experience. By no measure could anyone who has read the novel be able to say the film is a conscientious adaptation. *Curse* telescopes the action and changes the plot, the ending and the characters. The film is textually dialogic; it is the ultimate or final result of the adaptation of multiple sources that script writer, director and creative personnel have adapted into the narrative. While the opening credits proclaim that it is an adaptation of Mary Shelley's book, it is much more than this, and it shocked and appealed to an audience in a way that a 'faithful' adaptation would not have done.

The film has a complex relationship with this source novel and the idea of an adaptation is itself complex. 'Adaptation' is a charged word and the meaning and implications of the adapting process are contested. For many years adaptation theorists were concerned with the idea of 'fidelity', and adaptation studies themselves were hidebound by the so-called 'fidelity paradigm', which compared the faithfulness of a cinema adaptation to a source book, and mostly engaged in criticism of adapting works that transgressed too much from the source work.

Transgression is at the heart of *The Curse of Frankenstein* in both its plot and its creation. The first words we hear the Baron speak are to the priest: 'Keep your spiritual comfort for those who think they need it', he brusquely tells the clergyman. The Baron rejects the priest and his teachings, placing him beyond the controlling influence of religious beliefs, as do his unholy experiments. Frankenstein is a fornicator, a murderer, a tomb robber, a violator of the laws of nature as he refuses to let the dead stay dead. In short, the protagonist and titular character of the film is a transgressor against law and morality, and in this the character intersects neatly with the transgressive nature of the film itself.

In this chapter I will put these ideas on adaptations, be they faithful or transgressive, worthwhile or worthless, in a broader context of adaptation and the production history of Hammer. The way the Hammer team approached making their adaptation of Shelley's novel can be refocused away from criticising lack of fidelity to recognising the film as an instance of what Peter Brooker (2007: 110) calls a 'more intensively… ironic and self-reflexive' set of adaptations from sources such as classic literature. Adaptation theory itself has developed in enriching directions, moving past the traditional emphasis on studying the fidelity of a film adaptation to a source novel into more adventurous areas, including embracing the idea of a 'transgressive adaptation' and the manner in which an adapted work departs from the source. Far from looking for fidelity, theorists now consider the ways that a transgressive adaptation produces a work of cultural interest. Moving past and beyond the once dominant binary model of examining a book made into a film, and judging how faithful the resulting film was to the book, has also given us the critical apparatus to evaluate the points of differences as much as the points of similarities between an original work and the adapted work.

HAMMER STUDIOS AND ADAPTATION

Adaptation is essential to understanding Hammer in general, not just *Curse of Frankenstein*. Eventually Hammer's company name became synonymous with horror. But some of the films made by the 'old dark house' of Hammer seem to not quite belong. By the 1970s the company's gothic horrors were becoming box office failures but other films including *On the Buses* (1971), *Mutiny on the Buses* (1972), *Holiday on the Buses* (1973), *Love thy Neighbour* (1973) and *Man About the House* (1974) were much more successful. They were adaptations in a two-fold manner. They adapted from the original television situation comedies that were then ratings successes on British television. But they also adapted from the trend then prevailing in British cinema of making film adaptations of successful television shows. These films are a reminder of the extensive adaptations that Hammer carried out. These cheerful comedies can seem weird anomalies, out of step with the prevailing gothic horrors. But they are nothing of the sort; they are reminders of the central most important creative impulse in Hammer to adapt from as many sources as possible.

Works examining Hammer horror have gained momentum since Pirie's influential and ground breaking *Heritage of Horror* but have tended to consolidate a particular narrative that leaves this adaptation to the side. While Pirie's book was not specifically about Hammer, as a survey text on British horror cinema he did have a great deal to say about the company and devoted an entire chapter to Terence Fisher. Since then books and more recently serious academic journal articles have appeared, alongside a continued interest in the company and its output in trade journals and fan writings. But a major aspect of the company – and by extension their first gothic horror – continues to escape serious or sustained scrutiny: the adaptation process. *The Curse of Frankenstein* is the best place to consider this adaptive impulse. Looking at the film as a product of adaptation and as particularly intertextual adaptation, meaning that it is a work that draws simultaneously on many different sources, not just Shelley's novel, allows us to understand major aspects of the film's production, themes and reception, but ultimately leads to deeper understanding of Hammer in general.

Hammer's greatest successes and its astonishingly varied output are the result of adaptation. Early successes after the company's 1940s revival were the trilogy of Dick Barton films, *Dick Barton: Special Agent* (1948), *Dick Barton Strikes Back* (1949) and *Dick Barton at Bay* (1950). The films were adapted from the popular BBC Light Programme radio serial that ran from 1946 to 1951. From there the company plundered from a diverse range of sources. Some of Terence Fisher's earliest work for Hammer involved adaptation: his 1953 film *Spaceways*, which combined science fiction elements with a romance and a murder mystery, was adapted from a popular radio serial. Other radio serials including 'P.C. 49', 'Meet the Rev' and 'Life with the Lyons' were all adapted for scripts (Miller, 1995: 44). The studio scored major successes in the 1950s with its two Quatermass films, *The Quatermass Xperiment* (1955) and *Quatermass 2* (1957). These were again borrowed plumes, courtesy of the BBC and the television serials written by Nigel Kneale and produced by Rudolph Cartier, broadcast live in 1953 and 1955.

Throughout its production history Hammer continued to be a studio whose output was contingent on adaptation, including not just the gothic classics by Shelley, Stoker, Conan Doyle, le Fanu and Stevenson, but novels by Dennis Wheatley (specifically *The Devil Rides Out*, which Fisher filmed in 1968, and *To the Devil, A Daughter*, Hammer's last horror in 1976) and even more unexpected directions such as 1971's *On the Buses*. Hammer also scored a major hit with this film and it was the most profitable released in Britain that year (Bright & Ross, 2001: 45). Hammer's managing director James Carreras after all declared that 'we'll make Strauss waltzes tomorrow if that's what people want' (cited in Harmes, 2014: 102). If he never quite got to make his waltzes, he did at least omnivorously consume from, borrow, steal, rip-off and adapt from anything that seemed popular or just provided the basis for a good idea. Classical mythology relating the history of Medusa the Gorgon was the basis of Fisher's 1964 *The Gorgon*. Other sources adapted ranged from Russell Thorndyke's *Dr Syn* novels, that were used to make *Captain Clegg* (with Peter Cushing playing the fake vicar) in 1962 to J. Sheridan le Fanu's *Karmilla*, the vampire story which provided the subject matter of Hammer's commercially successful soft-core lesbian trilogy *The Vampire Lovers*, *Lust for a Vampire* and *Twins of Evil* of 1970 and 1971.

To the very end of Hammer's commercial life in the late 1970s, adaptation remained a central aspect of their output. The company's last gasp at the box office was 1978's *The Lady Vanishes* an adaptation as remake of Alfred Hitchcock's critically and commercially successful 1938 film. Hammer's version was a dismal failure and killed off the ailing company, but it also indicates that the adaptive impulse remained with Hammer until the very end. But in 1956, long before decay set in, it was the turn of Shelley's *Frankenstein* to provide the adaptive substance for Hammer. *Curse* does directly adapt from the source novel, in terms of the contours of its plot, the naming and motivation of characters and the setting of the action, but also deviates wildly as much as it adapts and generated high levels of cultural interest in doing so.

ADAPTING FRANKENSTEIN

Like any film that, however loosely, tells the Frankenstein story, *Curse* adapts from the novel. Mary Shelley's 1818 novel has been a major source of adaptive impulses in general, but these are rarely faithful. The 1931 Universal *Frankenstein* was not the first cinematic adaptation and there had been versions of the story since Thomas Alva Edison's 1910 silent film, followed by the loose adaptation *Life Without Soul* from 1915 (which did retain the chase across Europe that Hammer and most other film adaptations excised)[4] and then 1920's *Il Mostro di Frankenstein*. The novel inspired even earlier adaptations and stage versions were being performed as early as the 1820s (Hand, 2007: 10). The creative (and commercial) impulse to adapt from Shelley's novel has been apparent from the inception of cinema, continued through the Universal cycle (which lasts up to *Abbott and Costello meet Frankenstein* in 1948), through the Hammer cycle to Kenneth Branagh's *Mary Shelley's Frankenstein* of 1994 and the yet more recent (2007) television film with Julian Bleach as the monster and Helen McCrory as Dr Victoria Frankenstein, a geneticist. At the time of writing, yet another adaptation has been announced to star Daniel Radcliffe as Igor (essaying a character played by Bela Lugosi from 1939's *Son of Frankenstein* rather than the novel) and James McAvoy as Victor von Frankenstein (Young, 2013). But there are many elements of the novel, such as Captain Walton's voyage, the encounter with the Irish magistrate Mr Kirwin, or the creature's first person narrative, that have not made it into any film adaptation.

A common denominator across these films is their problematic, transgressive relationship with the source novel. Even in just a 16 minute silent reel, Edison's version was able to adapt from more than the novel. The appearance of the creature itself and of the makeup worn by actor Charles Ogle borrowed heavily from contemporary theatrical imagery, and especially from the portrayal on the stage of Caliban, the debased creature from Shakespeare's *The Tempest* (Hand, 2007: 12). This recurring transgression is especially striking with Branagh's 1994 adaptation. Its title *Mary Shelley's Frankenstein* is a statement claiming authenticity and faithfulness, indicating to audiences that this film is the story as told by Shelley herself. Significantly the near contemporary adaptation of the Dracula story by Francis Ford Coppola was *Bram Stoker's Dracula*, again proclaiming an apparent fidelity of the film to the novel. These statements of fidelity to a long-dead author and their novel are strikingly at variance with the actual films. Branagh's film is not at all a story that could be described as 'Mary Shelley's' and nor is Coppola's *Dracula* exactly as Stoker told it. Instead there are many creative liberties, including an extensive backstory for Dracula and the idea that Mina is the reincarnation of Dracula's lost love.

APPROACHES TO SHELLEY

Shelley's book has been adapted, plundered, parodied, mocked and turned inside out. There have been adaptations for the stage, including Sally Netzel's *Frankenstein's Monster* (1972), Victor Gialanella's major Broadway flop of 1981, and the National Theatre's 2011 production directed by Danny Boyle. Yet even freer adaptations extend to 1967's *I'm Sorry the Bridge is Out, You'll Have to Spend the Night* and *Frankenstein Unbound* by Bobby Pickett and Sheldon Allman, or arguably even Richard O'Brien's *Rocky Horror Picture Show*. An updated version *Frankenstein Unbound* was created by science fiction writer Brian Aldiss (Martin, 2003). The comedic potential of the novel has inspired Mel Brooks's *Young Frankenstein* (1974), which was also a homage to the 1931 adaptation, down to the reuse of surviving props and sets that were still on the Universal back lot. Elements of the original story, mostly the core element of a mad scientist bringing a monster to life, have appeared in works otherwise as diverse as the regular *The Simpsons* Easter specials, in manga works and even in pantomime (Forry, 1990; Heffernan, 1997).

The sheer diversity of media in which adaptations have been made, the variety of tones and styles in approach and the bewildering range of national contexts and storytelling traditions from which these adaptations have emerged, all indicate the richness of the source novel as an inspiration. This diversity also indicates that adaptations of the novel transcend media-specificity, having been films, television and mini-series, plays, musicals and comics. The adaptations are also diverse in the tone, from the relatively serious efforts of Universal and Hammer (although even here the comedy eventually burst through with 1970's *Horror of Frankenstein*), to the ponderous Kenneth Branagh adaptation, which contrast with the comedy of Mel Brooks or Richard O'Brien.

The diversity of adaptations of Frankenstein and Hammer's place within them can be explained by certain key statements about the processes and results of adaptation. Adaptation theory is a productive way to understand the Hammer team's creative intentions with *Curse*, and the outcome of their work. The 'moment' of adaptation, the transformation of a source (such as a novel) into another work (such as a film) registers as a point of cultural interest and generates significant cultural capital (Hutcheon, 2006: 7-8). It also means that the adapting work proclaims its prior relationship with the source in terms of title, plotting, character and other aspects that may carry across.

'Fidelity' has long been a core aspect of the theoretical speculation on adaptation. This focus has limitations and is problematic in a number of ways. To think about the fidelity of an adapting work to a source immediately casts the former as a palimpsest of the latter, but one which will inevitably be an unfaithful adaptation. Particularly with works such as eighteenth or nineteenth-century novels, most of which are of a length that render them unfilmable in their entirety (and the fact that there has never been a full adaptation of *Frankenstein* is a case in point) it is impossible to make a faithful adaptation. Inherent in the once dominant intellectual model of the adaptation of a book into a film were value judgments of the 'fidelity' of the adaptation to the source and criticism of works that 'betray' the adapted work (Lowe, 2010: 99).

THE BOOK IS BETTER?

Being judgmental brings to mind a crucial aspect of how Curse has been received and discussed. In critical terms, we find *Curse* adrift in what Petley (1986: 98-119) refers to as the 'lost continent' of British cinema, or the films which have sometimes sat below critical view and almost always below critical respectability. Petley includes in the 'lost continent' the quota quickies and B films, as well as the James Bond films, the *Carry On* films, trash and sexploitation cinema such as the *Confessions* films, as well as Hammer horror. They are 'lost' in the sense that they have been undervalued or critically derided, even if collectively they are among the most commercially successful and visible aspects of British cinema for popular audiences. Although some definitions of 'trash' and exploitation include box office failure (Brottman; Hunter, 2013), Hammer films are not lost to audiences, but to a body of critical thought that privileges social realism above genre cinema and a faithful adaptation above a transgressive one.

When applied to *Curse*, but also to a host of other films, the fidelity paradigm is limiting in two particular ways. One is that it insists on the binary of a book being adapted into a cinematic screenplay. Standard accounts of adaptation privilege a linear or one-way process of adaptation: a book becomes a screenplay which then finally becomes a film. This model is simply not up to the task of understanding many adapted works, including *Curse of Frankenstein*. The other is that it will inevitably subordinate the film to the literary original, as the idea that the film must inevitably betray, or just not be as good, as the novel can hamper critical appreciation of adaptations in their own right. Critical opinion can subordinate the adaptation to the original. As one major bookseller (Waterstones) asserts: 'the book is always better', a clearly commercial judgment that is understandable in its context, but which is also a problematic statement. The interest aroused by the transgression from the original cannot be taken on board or interpreted if we are only looking for fidelity.

Recent writings about adaptations of all kinds have provided different ways to think about adaptation than just the linear progression from book to film. However a consistent idea in adaptation theory is, as Hutcheon says, that 'adaptations have an overt and defining relationship to prior texts' (2006: 3). Further, adapted works 'usually openly announce this relationship' (ibid.). Such is the case with *Curse*; the credits proclaim that it is adapted from Shelley's novel, but at a deeper narrative level, the film is consistently proclaiming the different sources that have fed into it.

THE CURSE OF FRANKENSTEIN AS AN ADAPTED AND ADAPTING WORK

There were a range of contrasting and sometimes competing influences at work on the team at Bray in the plotting, casting and production of *Curse*. These range from the textual to the cinematic. The film is richly intertextual, meaning it draws on a diversity of sources. Cushing's dandified aristocrat derives from the tradition of wicked aristocrats from British melodrama, not to mention other sources as well, some of which are subtly but tellingly alluded to. One visually arresting sequence of the Baron leaving to visit the municipal charnel house to buy eyeballs, and Fisher keeps the audience's attention fixed on the Baron's nifty little leather bag. As he exits the front door Fisher's camera tracks down to the bag dangling in his hand, and the scene cuts immediately to the Baron walking into the charnel house, the camera all the while following the bag, into the next scene when it is resting on a coffin in the charnel house. The sequence in its entirety shows Fisher's long experience in editing as the sequence is seamless, but there is also a telling sign of an adaptive influence: the small bag with the sharp instruments shows the influence of Jack the Ripper on the Baron's characterisation. Other influences range from the monster mash-ups of the 1950s, the records of crimes committed by

The Baron goes shopping

notorious anatomists such as Robert Knox, as well as the glossy costume dramas made by Gainsborough. But in no way does *Curse* faithfully adapt from any of these sources; it is indebted to them, it plunders from them, but also transgresses from them in tone, style and effect.

At the foundation of all influences is Shelley's novel, but the relationship between text and film is complex. Much of this adaptation reflects script writer Jimmy Sangster's pragmatism. He called his memoirs *Do you want it good or Tuesday?* (2009), a title that reflects his no-nonsense realisation that he was never going to let mere fidelity stand in the way of borrowing a good idea. Sangster's script adapts from Shelley's novel, but also transgresses wildly. The film condenses the narrative, removes entire characters and settings, changes motivations and even changes the ending, as is raised in chapter three. In Shelley's novel, Herr Frankenstein is a student of natural philosophy from Geneva studying at Ingolstadt, whereas in the film he is a privately wealthy nobleman. The action in Hammer's film was mostly confined to Baron Frankenstein's chateau, whereas Shelley's original is far more epic, moving from Geneva to Chamonix until finally Frankenstein pursues his monstrous creation across the world to Scotland and to the Arctic. Key characters from the novel such as Frankenstein's father are absent from the film, as are key events, such as the creation of a mate for the creature and the monster's killing of Frankenstein's wife on their wedding night. Certainly the film is an adaptation, but it pays bare lip service to its source novel. Where it does most strongly adapt is from other cinematic traditions. The core essentials of the story – a scientist imbuing a monstrous creation with life – do remain in the film, but otherwise this film is a highly transgressive work.

Intertextual dialogue, the bringing together of different textual influences, promotes and stimulates originality. Attempting to break open the confines of the fidelity paradigm, theorist Robert Stam has come up with alternative terms to understand what adaptation is and why writers may be motivated to resort to it, as adaptation could also be called: '…reading, re-writing, critique, translation, transmutation, metamorphosis, recreation, transvocalization, resuscitation, transfiguration, actualization, transmodalization, signifying, performance, dialogization, cannibalization, reinvisioning, incarnation, or reaccentuation.' (Stam and Raenga, 2008: 25). Several of these are deliciously appropriate to a film about Frankenstein and his monster, including transmutation, metamorphosis, cannibalization and incarnation. While Stam is using these words to think about the different and often transgressive and iconoclastic ways that texts can be adapted, the resulting film made at Bray is in its own way to be understood with these terms. Jimmy Sangster's screenplay cheerfully cannibalises what Hammer wanted from the novel, subjecting some of it to strange metamorphoses – the scruffy Krempe becomes a young and urbane man for example – and other terms are capable of similar application.

The result of course is not 'faithful'. The result is a film that stimulated critical reaction and commercial success by bringing different works into dialogue with each other. If we move on from considering an adaptation as having a prior relationship with just one source, or as being something either derivative or unfaithful, we reach a more productive idea of adaptation as organic and provocative. Something of this capacity for creation is captured by Sanders's notion that: 'Texts feed off each other and create other texts' (2006: 13-14). *The Curse of Frankenstein* appears to us as a work that comes out of a process of intertextual dialogue, where there is not one original source but rather there are multiple points of origin in dialogue with each other (Hutcheon 2006: 2). These move from Shelley's novel to other horror film traditions and to the conventions of period drama.

Conclusion

It would be limiting to think of *Curse of Frankenstein* as faithful or not to the novel. Nor is there an uncomplicated linear relationship from book to film, as what we see on screen in *Curse* is the result of multi-textual influences; the film adapts, but from much more than just Shelley's novel. *Curse* was an adaptation that critics hoped would be a one off. Horror films had been so very rarely made in Britain prior to 1956, and those made in Hollywood were often only shown in restricted sessions or were banned altogether, including Tod Browning's 1932 film *Freaks*, which the British Board of Film Censorship banned outright. But there was this native tradition of gothic literature, until then plundered by foreign film makers but which had been left untapped by British film makers. With these thoughts under our belt on the immediate creative and commercial context for Fisher's and Hammer's work, is now time to look in more detail at the film as an adapting work. It is time to move back from Britain, from Bray, and from the Hammer set, and to take attention to Switzerland, in 1816.

Footnotes

4.   Interestingly the chase across the Arctic and the final confrontation between the creator and his creature is the starting point of the 2014 film *I, Frankenstein* (directed by Stuart Beattie) before the narrative jumps to the future.

CHAPTER THREE: THE BOOK: ADAPTING SHELLEY

Describing *The Curse of Frankenstein* as an adaptation of the 1818 novel *Frankenstein, or the Modern Prometheus* is a problematic point, even though the book clearly was of influence on at least some of the people making the film. Jimmy Sangster's script was both inspired by it and avoids it. The novel was being read on the set at Bray Studios, including by Sangster. Peter Cushing, who played Frankenstein more times than any other actor, was inspired by a range of sources. He consulted with a real doctor about the practicalities of brain surgery and also found inspiration in the accounts of the notorious nineteenth-century anatomist Dr Robert Knox, the employer of body snatchers Burke and Hare.[5] But Cushing also recalled in his memoirs that he the only way he could get a fix on the character and all its 'oddities and eccentricities' was to go back to the original source: the novel (Miller, 1995: 64; Dixon, 1991: 230).

But note Cushing was playing 'the Baron'; there is actually no such person of that rank in the original novel. One critical assessment of Peter Cushing's acting and his appearance in horror films described him as a 'frighteningly grey eminence' (Hutchinson, 1996: 86). The eminence alluded to is an apt description of the aristocratic bearing that Cushing brought to bear on his horror roles, especially playing the elitist dandy Baron Frankenstein. The literary Frankenstein eventually was a solitary figure, lost in the frigid and barren Arctic ice, a character far removed from the Baron of *Curse* who so clearly enjoys the comforts, not to say luxuries, of home life. The literary Frankenstein is an isolated and isolating figure, whereas Hammer's version is part of a social milieu. It is even established in the film that Frankenstein cannot operate his equipment on his own and he in fact must have a collaborator.

This aristocratic status is one of many deviations away from the source novel, and indicates from the outset that the relationship between the novel and Hammer film is complex and ultimately transgressive. But these transgressions, which ruthlessly condense plot, characters and dialogue, created cinematically suitable and satisfying alternatives to the original novel. Hammer created succinctness and cinematic impact in place of wordiness. Their approach to the novel is clear: it was a source ripe for commercial exploitation, not for faithful adaptation. By 1956 the book had long since been in the public domain, but the 1931 Universal film, notably its script and makeup design, was not. Universal tried to stop Hammer registering the film title *Frankenstein* in the United States and issued threats to the small British company that they would sue if the Universal take on *Frankenstein* was appropriated in any way. As a consequence was Hammer forced to look back past the 1931 film and take their inspiration from the novel?

The opening credits acknowledge that it is an adaptation from the 'classic story by M. Shelley'. But beyond that opening credit no other claims to textual fidelity are made, even if the credits are talking up the classic status of the book. The fact that Cushing is playing a Baron alerts us to the nature of this adaptation and its looseness. The very first line of chapter one in the novel (the first chapter of Frankenstein's narrative and thus after the three epistles by Captain Walton) says that 'I am by birth a Genevese, and my family is one of the most distinguished of that republic' (Shelley, 1985: 31). The line instantly distances the literary Frankenstein and his background from European aristocracy and locates him amongst the republican syndics of the Helvetic confederation. Later in the novel Elizabeth rather smugly reminds Victor that the 'republican institutions of our country have produced simpler and happier manners than those which prevail in the great monarchies that surround it'. Thus their serving girl Justine was more like one of the family, as a 'servant in Geneva does not mean the same thing as a servant in France and England' (Shelley, 1985: 63). In this moment Mary Shelley is very much writing as the daughter of her radical and free-thinking father William Godwin, but this talk of republican sensibilities finds no place in *Curse*, where a servant girl exists to be sexually exploited by a louche aristocrat. Even while they are covertly making love Victor insists that Justine address him as 'Baron'. He later contemptuously brushes off the now-pregnant Justine's demand that he marry her and suggests she finds a local boy in the village instead who will 'do just as well'. The film constantly refers back to class distinctions. Justine is left to simmer with jealousy when Elizabeth arrives and announces her engagement to Victor; in the same moment Victor casually tosses his top hat and cape to Justine, ignoring his concubine to make polite conversation with his fiancée. The characterisation of the Baron, his relationships with supporting characters including tutor and fiancée, his aristocratic as opposed to republican status and his interior milieu rather than his Alpine setting are all marked points of departure between novel and film that merit more detailed analysis. We start with the setting.

TRANSGRESSIONS: SETTING

The *mise-en-scene* in *Curse* is almost entirely based on the interior of the Baron's grand house, a focus at odds with the original novel. Mary Shelley conceived of the original idea for her story when staying in the Alps in the early-nineteenth century with Percy Shelley, Lord Byron and Dr John Polidori, Byron's personal physician (Macdonald, 1991). The subsequent novel is heavily descriptive of the beautiful alpine Swiss scenery, from Frankenstein's trips to Geneva and back, the creature's appreciation of the beauty of nature, and the pursuit of the creature through meadows and hills. The gardens around Bray were extremely versatile, becoming in time to represent India (in Fisher's *Stranglers of Bombay*) and Egypt (*The Mummy*) and endless middle European villages, but even Hammer's legendary design ingenuity couldn't stretch to recreating the Alps in Berkshire. The only glimpse of anything scenic is the brief outdoor scene of the murdered Professor's funeral procession, where the background is an unconvincing matte painting of some snowy mountains.

Sangster's script excises the panorama of the novel. After the opening titles have faded, the first shot is of a priest on horseback riding towards a forbidding looking prison in the distance. The priest rides against an alpine background that was achieved via another matte shot. However this glimpse of the wide outdoors is fleeting. Seconds into the film's running time the priest reaches the gateway of the prison and enters. His arrival allows Terence Fisher to display one of the most characteristic aspects of his film direction: action captured by a static camera and framed by a doorway, in this case the imposing gateway into the prison. It is not just the framing and camera positions that set the tone of the film, so does the action that is taking place. There is a rapid transition from the outdoor alpine world to the dark interior of the prison, as the priest enters, and is taken into the depths of the prison to meet Baron Frankenstein. From then on, the remainder of the film takes place in dark, interior spaces. In the film Frankenstein does not journey to Geneva, to London, to Edinburgh and the Scottish highlands, to Ireland, or to the Arctic. He barely sets foot outside his own front door. The theatrical trailer for the film promised cinema patrons a glimpse inside a 'house of hell', a comment that reflects the inward focus of the movie.

The literary Frankenstein and his creation were sensitive to nature and the outside world, the former even quoting Wordsworth and mediating on the 'awful majesty' of Mont Blanc (Shelley, 1985: 95). The latter noted the flora and fauna around him after his 'birth'. Frankenstein's fiancée Elizabeth also gets in on the act, rhapsodising in a letter to Victor about the 'blue lake and snow-clad mountains' near their family home (Shelley, 1985: 63). Fisher's world is by contrast interiorised and claustrophobic. Aside from the occasional exterior shot of Oakley Court (a stately home near Bray) that doubles as the exterior of the Frankenstein chateau, we see almost nothing of the exterior of Frankenstein's house, such is the emphasis on the world within. Inside the house, many of the spaces are dark and cramped. In one specially virtuosic sequence at the end of the film the Baron goes round and round these spaces, lunging up the stairs, turning corners to get into this laboratory, round more corners to get onto the roof and then around the flying buttresses. Fisher's immaculately framed and closely edited sequence reinforces the tight, interior spaces through which the Baron moves.

TRANSGRESSIONS: VICTOR FRANKENSTEIN

Not just the setting but the characters are also altered. Peter Cushing embodies a character markedly different from the literary original. At the most basic level, the 44 year old Cushing was significantly older than the young student of the novel (Meikle, 2009: 37). Cushing's energetic performance (including scaling the gibbet and the sprightly fight scenes and chase around the roof tops at the film's climax) more or less disguise the age difference, but there is certainly almost nothing of the young university student in Cushing's well-heeled aristocrat.

Nor is the vapid lifelessness of Shelley's Frankenstein apparent in Cushing's characterisation. The literary Frankenstein is listless where Cushing is dynamic. Early in the film it is made clear that the young Baron and the tutor have effectively changed places; the student outstrips the teacher in terms of energy and imaginative insight. Cushing's Baron is in charge of their study and their experiments and in an early scene when they reanimate the dead puppy, Frankenstein abruptly pushes Krempe's hand away and superintends the work himself. Throughout the film Fisher makes frequent use of close-ups of Cushing, whose bright blue eyes are in their way as visually arresting as all the red that is on the screen. Cushing brings astonishing energy to the part far removed from the effete and ultimately helpless character in the novel. Cushing is a bright and dynamic centre of the film in a way he could never have been if playing the effete weakling of the novel.

This effeteness shows in the way the literary Frankenstein responds to his creation. In the novel, once Frankenstein has animated his creation, he retreats from it in horror, falls asleep, returning to his home and hoping to never see the creature again. Throughout remainder of the novel Frankenstein is a tormented man, shattered by the deaths of friends and family members, struck down by mental and physical illness, and haunted by what he believes to be spectral visitations from his dead family who urge him on in his hunt of the monster across the Arctic, even as the hunt takes a terrible toll on Frankenstein's health. In some respects the role essayed by Colin Clive in the 1931 film comes closer to some of the descriptions of Frankenstein and his state of mind than Cushing's portrayal. Clive's highly strung, cackling and clearly demented scientist is reminiscent of the madman in the ice discovered by Captain Walton at the start of the novel. Cushing's character is clearly demented, in that he hopes to play god and create new life, but he also is poised, aristocratic, judicious and cunning. The literary Frankenstein was not only a denizen of a republic but tended to express his feelings and wear his heart on his sleeve. Cushing's character is coldly oblivious of his fiancée and indifferent about his marriage, when the literary Frankenstein offers reassuring and loving sentiments in letters to Elizabeth.

TRANSGRESSIONS: THE CREATURE

As the daughter of the radical thinkers William Godwin and Mary Wollstonecraft, Mary Shelley provides a strong literary underpinning to the novel derived from the writers valorised in her childhood home, including the seventeenth-century puritan writer John Milton. The impact of this literature vanishes in Sangster's screenplay. In the novel, the creature reads from a number of morally improving texts, including Milton's *Paradise Lost* as well as the classical Greek biographer Plutarch and the German poet Goethe and indeed he speaks in an exaggeratedly archaic and early modern style, informing Victor Frankenstein that 'thou art my creator'. In his final moments, the creature returns to this

Miltonic language when addressing Captain Walton, telling him 'Blasted as thou wert, my agony was still superior to thine' (Shelley, 1985: 215).

At a deeper ontological level, Milton's *Paradise Lost* and the relationship it delineates between the Maker and his creation informs Shelley's story. As Hindle points out, the reproachful tone of Adam's address to God in *Paradise Lost*, where Adam remarks 'Did I request thee, Maker, from my clay/To mould me Man/did I solicit thee/From darkness to promote me' encapsulates the fraught relationship between Frankenstein and the creature he has made but spurned (Hindle, 1985: xxvi). Later the creature (who has been reading Milton when hiding in the hovel next to the De Lacey's cottage) likens himself to the 'fallen angel' of Milton's poem (Shelley, 1985: 213). Shelley is clear that the tragedy of the creature's situation is twofold: he is hideous and therefore spurned; but he is endowed with sufficient insight and intelligence to perceive his ugliness and to understand he can never be loved. The creature in the novel is highly articulate and intelligent, not only reading Milton and Plutarch but being able to speak cogently. No such articulateness has defined the cinematic treatment of the monster. Karloff's creature could create sound, but mostly inarticulate grunts (although he did speak in 1935's *Bride of Frankenstein*). Sangster's screenplay for *Curse* went one further, and Christopher Lee's autobiography recalls his annoyance on getting the script and discovering that the monster had no dialogue at all (Lee, 1997: 249).

The creature of the novel was capable of premeditated and cunning action, most shockingly murdering Victor's brother and then Elizabeth, as well as deliberately planting evidence to incriminate Justine and cause her execution. His sheer brutal maleficence contrasts to Karloff's inadvertently tragic actions, such as throwing a little girl into a lake. Lee's actions as the monster seem more directly evil, to judge from the expression on his face when he bears down on the helpless old blind man but these are explained in the film as psychopathic impulses caused by brain damage, not the cunning of the literary monster. Lee also evokes considerable pathos in his performance. Towards the end of the film Krempe is brought in to see the creature, and by then it has been shot in the eye, been brain damaged, buried and resurrected, and looks even more hideous than ever because the Baron has partly shaved off its hair to operate on the brain. The creature turns away from Krempe, and seems to do so out of helpless embarrassment, but it is then forced by the Baron to 'perform' in a grotesque kind of show and tell, as it is made to sit and stand at the Baron's command. The scenes gain remarkable pathos if we remember that these pathetic actions are being performed by what remains of the 'finest brain in Europe' that Frankenstein cut out of the skull of the murdered Professor. Not only that but the hands belonged to the 'finest sculptor in Europe' but now they are only good for breaking sticks and snapping chains. The creature in the film has suffered horrendous brain damage, compared to the ugly but tragically articulate creature of the novel. The role makes full use of Christopher Lee's pantomimic ability and he resembles a marionette puppet with broken strings as he moves eloquently, but he is totally silent.

TRANSGRESSIONS: ELIZABETH, KREMPE AND THE SUPPORTING CAST

The supporting characters also differ from the novel to the film. Cushing's Frankenstein is assisted by a tutor, Paul Krempe. There is a Krempe in the novel, but this Monsieur Krempe is described as 'an uncouth man' (Shelley, 1985: 45), far removed from the dandy played in the film by Robert Urquart. Other characters such as the chemistry lecturer M. Waldman, are missing entirely, as are Frankenstein's great friend Henry Clerval (who is later murdered by the monster), his parents, his two younger brothers, the De Lacey family and Mr Kirwin. They have all vanished in Sangster's brisk contraction of the narrative. Also gone is the entire period of Frankenstein's sojourn at Ingolstadt University and his other travels.

Other major plot points of the novel are omitted or condensed. A servant called Justine does appear in the film and has an antecedent in the novel. However in the novel Justine was a sweet and good hearted girl wrongfully accused of murder and cruelly executed. In the film Justine is a girl of loose morals and is murdered by the monster. Speaking of murder, the entirety of the literary Frankenstein's family is missing from the film, as well as their terrible fates. In the book Frankenstein's mother dies of scarlet fever (Shelley, 1985: 42), his younger brother is murdered by the monster (who incidentally implicates Justine for the crime, leading to her execution) and his father, his health shattered by everyone he loves dying violently, expires towards the end of the novel. None of these characters appear in the film or are even mentioned, barring the parents who are both dead by the time we flash back to the Baron's childhood. In the novel

Frankenstein's fiancée Elizabeth is murdered on their wedding night, whereas in the film Elizabeth walks away from the cell, arm in arm with Krempe.

The relationship between Victor and Elizabeth is in fact one of the strongest points of transgression between the novel and the Hammer film. In the novel, the mutual love and affection between them is strongly emphasised (so much so that when she re-issued the novel in 1831 Shelley felt compelled to change Elizabeth's character from being Victor's cousin to being of no familial connection at all). Victor writes love letters and grieves violently for Elizabeth after her murder. He even feels haunted by his dead family, finding that their spectral immanence pushes him on in his quest to find and destroy the creature. Cushing's Frankenstein is coolly indifferent to Elizabeth, although one of the most subtly chilling suggestions in the film is the possibility that Frankenstein might one day cut her up and use bits of her in his experiments. 'Who knows my dear? Perhaps you will.... one day' says the Baron to Elizabeth after she expressed a hope to help him in his experiments. In the original script the line was intended as one of the more comedic, but its tone and impact were transformed by Fisher's serious treatment of the material and Cushing's subtle but chilling delivery (Meikle, 2009: 39).

NECESSARY CHANGES: DIALOGUE AND ACTION

The dialogue is another area where *Curse* differs from the novel. In many ways this is a blessing. When he eventually gains speech, the creature in the novel speaks in an elevated and high blown literary style indebted to his highbrow reading matter, but the spoken thoughts of other characters are even more florid. While the cast for *Curse of Frankenstein* included many highly talented actors, not least Peter Cushing, even they would have struggled to deliver some of Shelley's lines with any conviction or without tipping over into scenery chewing. Cushing is given terse and often blackly ironic dialogue, defined by its brevity, which is just as well. With Shelley's lengthy dialogue the film's narrative would have ground to a halt. Likewise, in the film the creature expires by plunging through a glass skylight into a vat of acid, with his clothes, hair and face aflame. How much more cinematically satisfying than if Sangster had tried to recreate the end of the novel, when the creature treats Captain Walton to a long speech on the misery of his existence.

CREATING ANEW

There are other aspects of the narrative which are not so much omitted in Sangster's screenplay, but which had to be created anew. Any reader who comes to the novel after seeing any of the film adaptations, be it Edison's 16 minute 1910 silent, Whale's 1931 effort, the Hammer film, the 1973 American television adaptation with James Mason and Tom Baker, or Branagh's sumptuous 1994 adaptation, may well be surprised that so many elements common to these cinematic adaptations, and seemingly so intrinsic to the Frankenstein story, are not actually in the novel. The novel is essentially a 'blank slate' in terms of the absence of any visual cues for the adaptor (Bonner and Jacobs, 2011: 40). There are, strikingly, no descriptions of what Victor Frankenstein actually looked like. Captain Walton's fourth letter noted that he had a foreign accent (to Walton's British ears) and his eyes had 'an expression of wildness and even madness' (Shelley, 1985: 25). Otherwise the character is a visual cipher.

Even more strikingly, there are few descriptions of what the monster looked like, nor of the process of its creation. There is a comment that the creature is 'hideous and my stature gigantic' and that it is 'distorted' (Shelley, 1985: 125) but otherwise the rest is left to the imagination. The horrified reaction of the two De Lacey children to seeing the monster (they scream and one of them faints) is also a good indication that there is something appalling about its appearance. But otherwise there are no accounts of surgical scars, robotic bolts, or obvious stitching that informs the cinematic portrayal of the creature, from Karloff's lumbering monster to Christopher Lee's makeup by Philip Leakey, which has been described as looking like a car crash.

A yet more striking absence for anyone encountering the novel after seeing the film, especially the Universal or Hammer versions, is the exceptionally low key creation scene in Shelley's book. Besides reading Milton and her father's own work, it is known that Mary Shelley was familiar with the work of the radical scientist Humphrey Davy and his writings on electricity. During the stay with Percy, Lord Byron and Dr Polidori there was also much talk of the experiments of Dr Erasmus Darwin and electrical galvanism (Hindle, 1985: xvi). Percy Shelley was himself fascinated by electricity and galvanism and one of his biographers Thomas Hogg recalled that Percy Shelley, while at Oxford University, had shown Hogg 'various instruments, especially the electrical apparatus;

turning the round the handle very rapidly, so that the fierce, crackling sparks flew forth' (Hogg, 1858 I: 33). As Hindle (1985: xxi) points out, this description is actually a close literary match for the many realisations of the monster's creation in film, including the 1931 Universal version and Hammer's own, where lightning crackles and sparks fly. In Hammer's film, the novelty of using colour film was exploited to great effect in the scenes of Cushing at work in his laboratory. The dual wheels of the Wimshurst machine caused lights to glow bright red when in operation, more red lights on a power board flared brightly and sparks flew around, all echoing Percy Shelley's excited experiments with his apparatus when a young man at university.

However if we seek any similar passages in the 1818 novel we are disappointed. There is admittedly a description early in Frankenstein's chapters of the narrative of his scientific curiosity about lightning and electricity, when the young Victor 'witnessed a most violent and terrible thunder-storm'. As Victor narrates to Captain Walton, 'I beheld a stream of fire issue from an old and beautiful oak…. so soon as the dazzling light vanished, the oak had disappeared, and nothing remained but a blasted stump' (Shelley, 1985: 40). No such level of description characterises the actual moment of creation later in Frankenstein's narrative. One paragraph, which opens chapter five, is all that Shelley provides by way of description, when Victor 'collected the instruments of life around me, that I might infuse a spark of being into the lifeless thing that lay at my feet'. Frankenstein succeeds after some hours work, and 'I saw the dull yellow eye of the creature open; it breathed hard, and the convulsive motion agitated its limbs' (Shelley, 1985: 56).

The follow-up to the creation is equally low-key, not to say anti-climactic. Having done the impossible, played god, become the modern Prometheus, Frankenstein's next step is to fall asleep. Again Sangster transgresses from this scenario in the novel; in his treatment of the story, the next stage after the monster awakes is more dramatic, as the creature goes mad and tries to throttle the Baron. The Hammer film historian Mark Miller is right to pinpoint the 'maddening dullness' of Shelley's literary Frankenstein, a character who sleeps, frets, wallows in a moral agony and who lets his wife get murdered by the creature because he was searching in the wrong room of the house (Miller, 1995: 55). He spurns his creation immediately, whereas in the film Peter Cushing looks like a proud father as he beholds the creature. In all vital respects the character created in Sangster's script and personified by Cushing differs greatly from Shelley's.

Accordingly there were elements that Shelley included, such the extensive intellectual speculation underpinned by her reading of Milton, Godwin and other authors, that film adaptations have eschewed. Then there those aspects not in the novel that film makers have had to introduce, including the set pieces of the monster's creation and animation through electricity. In this regard, *The Curse of Frankenstein* sits in a trajectory with other adaptations. There is certainly no room in Sangster's no nonsense screenplay for philosophical speculation about the relationship between a creator and his creation, or for heavy handed dialogue. The education which Baron Frankenstein is shown receiving in the film is similarly brisk and matter of fact. In the novel, the young Victor was originally entranced by the fifteenth and sixteenth-century writings of natural philosophers and high magicians such as Cornelius Agrippa, only to discover when at university that their theories and conclusions were long discredited. Hammer's Baron Frankenstein doesn't waste his time on out-dated and esoteric writings but rather an early montage sequence shows the young Victor (Hayes) and the slightly older version (Cushing) receiving a thoroughly grounded anatomical education from Krempe. The film inverts the novel's delineation of Victor's early immersion in outmoded scientific thought, as the young Baron, so he tells Krempe, has found his old tutor unsatisfactory because his reading and knowledge were at least 30 years out of date. In the film it is Victor, not his tutor, who hungers after new knowledge and disparages the old.

Conversely Sangster makes up for those things that Shelley does not provide, besides the creation scene. While she briefly mentioned Frankenstein having to visit a charnel house, Sangster's script actually takes us there, and to gallows, graveyards and sepulchres. The brief and laconic description of the creature coming to life in Shelley's novel is replaced by an extended and visually dramatic and colourful sequence of the creature being blasted into life by lightning.

CONDENSING NARRATIVE: SANGSTER AND THE NOVELS

As I have previously suggested, critical opinion on *Curse* tends to put it as the tentative start to the greater success of next year's *Dracula*. But Sangster's ability to turn a sprawling nineteenth-century novel into a compact 80 minute film is an ability that bursts forth fully developed with *Curse* and which repeats with *Dracula*. But the essential ability was there already with *Curse*. With his screenplay with *Dracula* Sangster again took a lengthy novel which, like Shelley's, comprised multiple authorial voices and different textual forms (letters, diary entries, newspaper reports and so on). Once again Sangster is ruthless. Out go entire plot lines (Dracula's trip to England and the action in Whitby, including the spooky arrival of the ship with the dead man strapped to the wheel are both missing). Also gone are entire characters. Dracula's three wives become one; Dr Seward, his fiancée, the fly-eating Renfield and others have all vanished. But Sangster also creates anew. In Stoker's original novel, Harker had arrived at Castle Dracula with the rather prosaic task of cataloguing the Count's library. In Sangster's script he has come with the much more dynamic and cinematically interesting intention of murdering the Count. The changes, the cuts and the additions work together to produce an admittedly superb film adaptation of *Dracula*. Combined with Fisher's judicious camera work and his immense experience as an editor, the 1958 film is a taut and powerful version that arguably has not been bettered by later and more lavish versions. But the script is the basis of it all and this script is simply the second iteration of a talent that Sangster showed he had all had fully at his command in *Curse*'s script, where he could cut, amend and add to create something that worked on screen.

DEBTS TO THE NOVEL: STRUCTURE

And yet we cannot regard Sangster's script for *Curse*, or Fisher's realisation of it, as wholly eschewing the novel. If we look deeper, influences reveal themselves. One is the structure of the film itself, which is non-linear and told in flashback. In this regard, it is notably different from the 1931 Universal version, which after a brief introduction from Edward van Sloan (who appears from behind a curtain to fore-warn the audience not to get too frightened) is told through a linear narrative progression. By contrast, Sangster takes us to the story through non-linear means. It starts at the end, with the disgraced Baron in a prison cell, awaiting execution for murder. We end up there again at the very end of the film, having come full circle and the Baron is led off to execution. In the meantime the Baron has told his story to the priest, moving back in time to his childhood and then forward in time to more recent events that have climaxed in the murder of the serving maid Justine and the destruction of the creature.

Sangster's narrative is actually emulating one of the most striking literary features of the 1818 novel: its onion-ring structure. Shelley's novel is notable for its dramatic intimacy; the narrators all see each other through each other's eyes as Walton describes Frankenstein, who in turn narrates the birth of monster, and the monster recounts his own sightings of Frankenstein and his family. The novel begins in epistolary form (showing that besides Milton and Godwin, Shelley had likely been reading the great eighteenth-century novelists such as Samuel Richardson) with Captain Walton's letters from his ship back to his sister. From these the novel moves into Frankenstein's first person narrative recounted to the Captain. Then at the core of Frankenstein's narrative come several chapters of the monster's own narrative, which is in terms of the novel's narrative relayed back to Frankenstein who in turn relayed it to the Captain. On the other side of the creature's narrative the novel returns to Frankenstein's first person narrative, until we end up back where we started with Captain Walton writing a letter to his sister, now recounting the death of Frankenstein and the disappearance of the creature in the arctic wastes. The structure of the 1957 film is not so complex, beginning in the cell, flashing back to Frankenstein's childhood, then his adulthood, till finally we come back to the cell and the priest. Also, in contrast to the multiple authorial voices that are in the 1818 novel (Walton, the creature, Victor and sometimes Elizabeth as well, whose letters are quoted) the only authorial voice in the film in Baron Frankenstein's. However the structure of the framing narrative, and the use of the flashbacks, take their point of origin from the 'onion-rings' of Shelley's novel.

By thinking of the complex ways the film intersects with and deviates from the novel, we can start to liberate the film from the mass of critical opinion which sees it as a faltering first step before the triumph of 1958's *Horror of Dracula*. The opening narration, the super-text on the screen and above all the framing narrative in the prison cell announce the film's prior relationship with the novel. Words (in vivid red) flash up on the screen and we read: 'more than a hundred years ago, in a mountain village in Switzerland, lived a man whose strange experiments with the dead have since become legend. The legend is still told with horror the world over. It is the legend of the THE CURSE OF FRANKENSTEIN'. They suggest Sangster's emulation of the famous onion-rings whereby Shelley leads the reader deeper and deeper in the plot and to the relationship between the creature and its creator. The use of this opening title-card with the back story has been singled out by some commentators as evidence of the tentative and less successful nature of this film compared to the next year's *Dracula* but this judgement can be re-oriented, if we consider that this opening is one aspect of the adroit transformation into cinematic form of the novel's structure. While Sangster jettisons much of this depth and subtlety, and almost all of the philosophical speculation, he does take us deeper into the narrative by means of this structure.

NOVEL INTO FILM: THE GOTHIC TRADITION

The novel that *Curse* adapts from is itself drawing off multiple sources, from Milton's seventeenth-century epic *Paradise Lost* (not to mention the classical epics that in turn had informed Milton's style and narrative and the notion of Frankenstein as a 'second Prometheus') to works on electricity by Humphrey Davy and natural sciences by Erasmus Darwin and Luigi Galvani, on natural philosophy by Jean Jacques Rousseau, as well as the radical ideas imbibed at home from her parents. As Hand points out, the Frankenstein character in the novel is himself experimenting with adaptation in the way he is metamorphosing body parts into a new creation, but the book itself is a work of intertextual adaptation (Hand, 2007: 9). It is a complex work in terms of the influences it synthesises.

Equally complex is the nature of the relationship between *Curse* and the novel. The film's structure and its text-heavy opening are both adaptations into cinematic terms of the structure of the novel. But where it adapts the film also leaves out many aspects, and adds others not found in the novel. Throughout its running time, the film proclaims its prior relationship with the novel, from the title and titular character, to the basic contours of the plot. One of the clearest parallels is that both the film and the novel move to a dramatic climax on the eve of Victor's wedding to Elizabeth. But it transgresses in the way it is plotted, in the way it presents its central character and the supporting characters and their relationships, and in what it either leaves out or creates anew, in contravention of the novel. Even if the dramatic movement towards the wedding is a point in common, even here the film diverges from the book; in the book the creature malevolently and deliberately kills Elizabeth but in the film she walks away from the carnage arm in arm with Krempe.

But has there ever been a faithful adaptation of *Frankenstein, or the Modern Prometheus*?
Even the subtitle of the novel, which adds a richly layered set of associations to the
novel (Raggio, 1958), to the ambitions of the titular character and in terms of the
literary, religious and mythical antecedents that were running through Mary Shelley's
mind, is a layer of depth that no film has captured. In its own way the 1931 adaptation
leaves out and creates anew. Despite claiming to be *Mary Shelley's Frankenstein*,
Branagh's was arguably more in line with Fisher's 1957 work. Notably Branagh included
a lengthy creation scene, showing the creature emerging from amniotic fluid, which
has no precedent in Mary Shelley's book but does in Fisher's film. In 1968 the Thames
Television series *Mystery and Imagination* attempted a faithful retelling of the novel,
with Ian Holm starring as both Frankenstein and the creature. If we try to judge fidelity
in terms of how much of the novel is included in the adaptation, then this version
may be the most faithful. Frankenstein attends university, is lectured by M. Krempe, his
maid Justine is implicated for the murder of Frankenstein's younger brother, and there
are other sequences from the novel that have rarely made it into other adaptations.
However there is still no trip to England, Scotland and Ireland, no chase across the arctic
ice, no Captain Walton and certainly no Alpine scenery in a television production that
was entirely made in a studio. The sheer scale of the novel defeats full adaptation.

Or does it? A central issue raised by adaptation is the question of choice. Adapters
make choices about what to remove, what to keep in, and what to create anew. Any
adaptation therefore is not necessarily or not at all a compromised or pale imitation
of a literary source, but a result of choices. A classic novel especially, one from the
eighteenth or nineteenth century, presents adapters with a number of choices, such is
the length of the narrative, the diversity of locations or the proliferation of characters
in a work such as Henry Fielding's *History of Tom Jones a Foundling* or Charles Dickens's
Great Expectations, or indeed *Frankenstein*. Sangster and then the remainder of the
Hammer team chose to make a taut, tense and claustrophobic thriller, with a minimum
of distractions away from Cushing's intense scientist.

Ultimately the most significant question about choice in adaptation is the question
of genre. In the novel, the rhapsodising about nature, the republican sympathies, the
allusions to Goethe, all position *Frankenstein* as a Romantic text and Shelley as a child of
the Enlightenment. While some scholars such as Brian Aldiss have attempted to position

the novel as an early science fiction story, we can still say that it is not a horror story. Yet it could be adapted into a horror film. *Curse* took the essentials of the story and added those things – the laboratory, the bodies, the eyeballs, the violence, the hideousness - necessary to make it horror. Whale's film had contained some grotesque elements, but these were the mannered grotesqueries of Expressionism rather than the direct surgical horrors of *Curse*. Hammer's achievement in making the Frankenstein story into a horror story, which is the way it has been seen since, is a reminder of why we need to strip away the weight of later traditions and see the power of its innovation.

CONCLUSION

When James Carreras first registered the title for his proposed film in 1956, he set of figurative alarm bells at Universal, who threatened a lawsuit should anything done by Hammer emulate the 1931 *Frankenstein*. Some historians have seen the result of this threat as forcing Hammer to go back to the novel, as it was safely in the public domain. But this resort to the novel was at best qualified. There are the core elements of the story: a mad scientist; a creature; Switzerland; and a fiancée called Elizabeth. But in almost every other respect, the film is daringly different from the novel. It contracts and interiorises a book that straggled in its narrative and was fixated on the outdoor panorama of Swiss scenery. Justine moves from being a virtuous victim executed by the state to a vamp murdered (and perhaps raped) by the monster. Whole characters, episodes and sequences are removed or changed beyond recognition, such as the dishevelled M. Krempe becoming the young and attractive Paul Krempe. Frankenstein in the film does not have the family of the novel, nor does Cushing's character attend university, nor read widely in antiquated works of natural philosophy as does the literary original. Having examined the relationship of novel to text, it is now time to return from Shelley's visit to Geneva with Byron and Polidori and return to film studios.

FOOTNOTES

5.   In 1959 Cushing played Knox in The Flesh and the Fiends.

CHAPTER FOUR: CINEMA PART 1: HORROR BEFORE HAMMER

The Hammer name is one of the most prominent in the history of horror cinema, but *The Curse of Frankenstein* was not created in a vacuum, in terms of what was happening at Bray, in the wider British film industry, and in Hollywood. Both Terence Fisher and his creative environment are suffused with questions of adaptations from prior cinematic achievements. In taking perceptions and focus off the twenty years of film production that came *after* the release of *Curse* and re-orienting attention back to the film itself and its creative context, we will see clearly why and how it adapts from cinema, and understand how that adaptation created a work of shocking novelty. *Curse* appalled critics, but little has been said about why it shocked, and its relationship with the horror films preceding it in British cinemas, including native British cinema and American imports. By considering it as the starting point for a tradition of twenty years' worth of film production, as many writers have done, overlooks what was regarded as its novelty.

There are many 'firsts' wrapped up in *The Curse of Frankenstein*. It was the first of Hammer's gothic horrors, the first to team Fisher, Lee, Cushing and the rest of the Hammer crew, the first of many sequels, the first Frankenstein movie in colour, and the first Frankenstein film made in Britain. But it did not emerge from nowhere. It is now time to give more detailed attention to where it came from, in commercial and creative terms and the film's relationships with earlier films.

Hammer's chief executive James Carreras has been praised for his business acumen (including signing distribution deals simultaneously with every major US studio) and derided for vulgarity and crassness. His technicians and actors were bucking a trend in making gothic horror but doing so successfully. Circumventing and in fact inverting the normal commercial implications of getting an X certificate is one indication of this point, as is the original decision to make a Frankenstein film. Where did it come from? What brought Lee, Cushing, Fisher and Hammer together? To answer these questions we leave Bray for a time, going back further and to different studios.

It seemed that by the 1950s horror films and the genre in its entirety had outstayed their welcome. Most histories of Hollywood and British horror situate the 1950s as a nadir of horror production, with films made on poverty row by washed up stars, or else done on the cheap by Universal. This narrative is well-entrenched, particularly in the juxtaposition of a 'golden age' of 1930s horror with the low point of early 1950s. But these critical assessments overlook that there was still a paying audience for horror features into the 1950s. Hitherto the immediate background to *Curse* has been located with Hammer's own early genre efforts, especially the Quatermass films. So far historians of the company have not linked the company's first gothic horror with the much maligned but still profitable horrors being made in Hollywood. But if we do, suddenly things fall into place: why Hammer decided to venture into gothic cinema; why they decided at first to make a black and white comedy horror; and the market they were trying to tap into.

SOME PROGENITORS: GOTHIC

As Peter Hutchings and David Pirie have both pointed out, horror cinema that is quantifiably 'gothic' takes that name and its defining characteristics from literature, notably the gothic novels of the eighteenth and nineteenth centuries. The definition of any work as gothic is fraught with contested meanings, even if there is at least agreement among scholars on a core body of texts from the eighteenth and early nineteenth centuries that comprise a gothic canon, including Matthew Lewis's *The Monk*, Mrs Radcliffe's *Castle of Otranto* and *The Mysteries of Udolpho* (1794), Godwin's own gothic work *St Leon*, and, of course, *Frankenstein*. There is also Sophia Lee's *The Recess* (1783–5) and Mary Wollstonecraft's *The Wrongs of Women* (1798). These novels and texts pursue a number of trajectories that continued into nineteenth-century works, notably *Dracula* and a number of Robert Louis Stevenson's works such as *Dr Jekyll and Mr Hyde*, although scholars are increasingly alert to the number of expressions of gothic themes across the century, even in Marx's *Das Capital*, which is full of gothic metaphors and allusions to the uncanny, such as hobgoblins and werewolves (Policante, 2010: 2). Gothic novels comprise of a range of preoccupations and settings, and Sedgwick (1986) suggests that some of them are religious institutions, subterranean spaces, burials and the unspeakable as typical features of gothic novels. Some of these do appear in *Curse*.

If we say that Sangster and the rest of the team of the adapted from a 'gothic; novel, this statement brings into view a complex trajectory from the source text to the film. The

The final confrontation is framed by gothic spaces

script and production design together create a richly gothic world. The Baron's chateau is a world of rich luxury but also dark chambers. The climax of the film shows the Baron and the creature chasing each other around the gothic flying buttresses of the roof space.

Another delicious gothic touch comes shortly before the Baron murders the visiting Professor Bernstein. The Baron invites the Professor to inspect a painting hanging on the landing: 'It was purchased by my father and illustrates one of the early operations', says Frankenstein. In his analysis of the film, Wheeler Winston Dixon says that they are looking at a nondescript painting but that's not right; actually the picture is the 1632 oil painting 'The Anatomy Lesson of Dr Nicolaes Tulp' by Rembrandt. The painting shows the dissection of an executed criminal and is a closely detailed and gruesome depiction of the corpse's anatomy. Details such as these enrich the gothic atmosphere of the film.

But this gothic potential had not previously been exploited by a British studio. Most of the landmarks literary texts that have been influential as adapted sources are British (if that is taken to include Stoker and le Fanu before the establishment of the 1922 Irish Free State) but earlier horror films had been made by Universal Studios in Hollywood. Such is David Pirie's point in *A Heritage of Horror*, where he suggests that British horror films take their inspiration and textual sources from a body of native British texts and traditions. Pirie's point was part of a wider body of arguments he deployed to build a case for taking British horror cinema seriously, which at the time he wrote in 1973 was far from being a common critical or academic position. While partly polemical, his argument remains valid, as especially in the case of Shelley and Stoker, but also Conan Doyle and le Fanu, major works that have been adapted have been by British writers, even if there works have been set in non-British locations including Switzerland and Transylvania.

But there was also an irony underpinning Pirie's argument, in that these native British literary traditions had been appropriated by foreign film makers, mostly the horror specialists working at Universal Studios in the 1930s. Even here we must be cautious in seeing cultural divides. Notably the 1931 adaptation of Frankenstein was made in America, by an American studio and with American money, but the director (James Whale) and its stars (Boris Karloff and Colin Clive) were British. But overall the irony stands that Hollywood, mostly Universal, plundered long-dead British writers to make their horror films and appropriated from a British literary heritage.

In the same year as Whale's *Frankenstein*, 1931, Universal also made an adaption of Stoker's *Dracula* (or more accurately an adaptation of the theatrical adaptation of the original book). Hollywood also later made adaptations of Stevenson's *Dr Jekyll and Mr Hyde* and a version of his *Body Snatchers* and Conan Doyle's most gothic Sherlock Holmes story, *The Hound of the Baskervilles*. Universal exploited to a degree this literary heritage. Wheeler Winston Dixon describes Terence Fisher as the 'John Ford of horror cinema'; the comment has some meaning in terms of the way Fisher and his Hammer collaborators clawed back national ownership of their literary heritage.[6] If Ford's westerns were deeply embedded in American national archetypes and foundational narratives, then Fisher's first Hammer is a statement of British re-appropriation of a lost cultural heritage, but also a source of adaptation never before used by British film makers.

Curse may be gothic, but its adaptation from the gothic literature comes via other mediating sources that stand between the original gothic texts and the film. From Mrs Radcliffe, Horace Walpole to Matthew 'Monk' Lewis and then Shelley, to Robert Louis Stevenson, J. Sheridan le Fanu, Arthur Conan Doyle and Bram Stoker later in the nineteenth century, 'gothic' as a term became synonymous with a number of characteristics. One is the uncanny, or the appearance of things, objects, situations or people that promote feelings of dread or uncertainty. These uncanny things often appeared in against backdrop of dark underground spaces, mouldering castles, frightening monasteries or sepulchres and graveyards, including the Frankenstein family vault. But this body of British literature mostly chose to locate the uncanny gothic horrors outside the British Isles, from Transylvania (obviously) to Geneva to castles and convents in France and Germany (Harmes, 2014). The titular Castle of Otranto in Walpole's 1764 novel was set in medieval Italy.

PROGENITORS: GOTHIC CINEMA

Mention of gothic source texts reminds us of two important points. One is that any film about Frankenstein is an adaptation, taking inspiration from the 1818 novel but also from the very considerable cultural baggage that has accumulated around Shelley's work. The other is that even as relatively early (in film making terms) as 1956, there was already a fairly extensive film making tradition within the horror genre based in Hollywood. But gothic horror's place within the British film industry and more broadly within British society was complex.

Not only does *Curse* normally play second fiddle to Hammer's own *Dracula* of the next year, but it also languishes in the shadow of Universal's 1931 movie. If Christopher Lee may be the definitive Dracula (certainly the cinematic representation of vampires with fangs belongs to him, not to Lugosi's Dracula), his Creature has nothing of the spectacular afterlife and recognition factor of Karloff's from the 1931 film. Karloff's flat headed, neck-bolted lumbering creature (which does not take inspiration from Shelley's descriptions) is the definitive representation of Frankenstein's monster, repeated in sequels (sometimes played by Karloff, as in 1935's *Bride of Frankenstein* and other times with the role taken by lesser talents such as Lon Chaney Jnr) and endlessly in parodies, from *The Munsters* to *Frankenweenie*. In comparison, Hammer's monster make up, while effective and testament especially to Phil Leakey's ability to improvise and produce impressive results on a small budget (a skill he shared with everyone else working at Bray) has not been nearly so enduring in popular consciousness.

The very obvious visual distinction between Karloff and the Universal Studio look and Hammer's monstrous aesthetic indicates the ambiguous and complex relationship between the 1931 film and *Curse*. Commercially and creatively (and who can say how separate these are) the Hammer film is not a palimpsest of the 1931 Universal *Frankenstein*. Commercially, it couldn't be. Universal Studios threatened legal action if Hammer included any scene, design or character that was in the 1931 film but not in Shelley's novel. In 1956, Universal's 1931 film remained a current and well known property. In the US it was routinely repeated on television and the bullet-neck iconography of Boris Karloff's creature remained enduringly potent and popularly known. Universal was thus not defending a film that was over 25 years old, but something that remained known through repeats and through sequels and was still a viable commercial property.

Creatively the film differs from the 1931 version in the choices Sangster made about which scenes and characters to delete, choices which differed to Universal's own condensation of the novel's plot. Visually Whale's vision wholly differs from Fisher's. The 1956 and 1931 films are significantly different in the way different characters are foregrounded and emphasised. One reason Karloff's monster make up remains such a signature creation (besides the fact that it is brilliant) is that the monster is the focus of Whale's 1931 film. The film is arguably responsible for one of the most familiar confusions about Mary Shelley's story in modern popular culture: that it is the monster itself that is called Frankenstein (the title of the 2014 release *I, Frankenstein* is a recent restatement of this confusion). The 1931 places its focus on the creature, ineluctably associating a name – Frankenstein – with an image – Karloff in his make-up. The character of the scientist, played in Whale's film by Colin Clive, is a subordinate character compared to the monster. Hammer inverted this relationship. Lee's monster does not appear until the latter part of the film, and throughout the entire film the focus is on Peter Cushing's poised, energetic scientist. Cushing steals the show. He was an energetic actor, moving constantly around a film set; Lee tended to remain still and only move when necessary. Overall it is Cushing who captures and holds attention with his icy performance and his finely crafted details and nuances, from the way he expertly wields the antique surgical equipment to his fussy checking of times with his fob watch. Colin Clive had personified Dr Frankenstein as a gabbling, neurotic and above all deranged scientist. Cushing's Baron Frankenstein may still be a mad scientist, but he is altogether a more urbane, aristocratic and above all classier character than Clive's highly mannered characterisation. Whereas Clive's Frankenstein was assisted by a deformed dwarf, Cushing's is aided (to start with anyway) by the equally urbane and well-dressed figure of Paul Krempe. It is impossible to think of Clive's character having a social life or sitting down to make polite and sophisticated chit chat.

By contrast, *Curse* shows an altogether more rounded view of Frankenstein and the character grips and holds the audience's attention as a rounded, fascinating person. He raids charnel houses, murders people and reanimates the dead, but is also the perfect host (until he throws his guest over the bannister rail) and has a taste for the finer things in life. In one sharply realised scene, the Baron and his wife sit down to a breakfast in their beautifully furnished dining room, pass each other delicately crafted cruets, and chat about the inconvenience of the sudden disappearance of their parlourmaid.

Pass the marmalade: the Baron and Elizabeth have to cope without their maid

The maid has been murdered by the deranged monster lurking upstairs and the scene, dripping in black humour, captures the sophistication of Baron Frankenstein that lies alongside his diabolical experiments. Almost as good is the jet black comedy of the conversation between the Baron and the Professor as they mount the staircase in the chateau just before Frankenstein pushes the professor off and steals his brain. Again we see the urbane and erudite Baron. 'I really am most honoured to have you here, sir', says Frankenstein, in a line that yields up more than one meaning as the Professor is a distinguished visitor, but Frankenstein also means that he is relieved to have at last found a suitable brain. In turn the Professor compliments the Baron for his charming home and its 'wonderful atmosphere', dialogue that is blackly ironic given that the Professor has only seconds to live because the Baron has coolly and cunningly arranged his murder.

Colin Clive's mannered performance finds no echoes in Cushing's more grounded if totally mad scientist. As Dixon has pointed out, the visual aesthetic of the films also contrast, in a way that reinforces the distinctions in style, expression and acting style between the Universal and Hammer iterations of the story and the actors starring in them. Clive's mad scientist operated in an environment and *mise-en-scene* that suited his mannered style. The sets were severely expressionist in character and harked back to German cinema of the previous decade (Dixon, 1991: 258). Cushing's laboratory is an earthier and more realistic setting, even down to the ambient sound, as the characters in Whale's film clambered around on echoing wooden rostrums, giving a rather shoddy theatrical impression compared to the solidity of Hammer's sets. Not only was the Wimshurst machine real and generated large amounts of electricity, the rest of Baron Frankenstein's equipment, the scalpels, the brass instruments, the charts and the anatomy tomes, gives the impression that you could actually do real medical work with them. These moments take us a long way from the babbling lunatic and his expressionist laboratory of the 1931 film and project us into a quite different film making tradition of Britain's period and costume dramas, of which more later.

COMEDY HORROR

The general trajectory of the Universal gothic horror films has been well told by a number of film historians, who follow mostly the same contours in the points they make. Generally they suggest that the original high standards of the 1930s Universal horrors, including Whale's *Frankenstein*, Tod Browning's *Dracula* (1931), Whale's *Bride of Frankenstein* (1935) and Rowland V. Lee's *Son of Frankenstein* (1939) gradually fell away (Crane, 1994: 75). While the original stars Boris Karloff and Bela Lugosi found their careers on the skids, Universal continued making horror films to diminishing returns, casting lesser actors such as John Carradine and Lon Chaney Jnr. in multi-monster films such as *House of Frankenstein* and *House of Dracula* (Hutchings, 2003: 22), which debased the former high standard of the films featuring Dracula, Frankenstein's monster, the Mummy and the Wolfman. Meanwhile smaller studios on the Hollywood 'poverty row' such as Monogram made cheap horrors, giving employment to former Universal stars such as Lugosi, and horror descended to the sensationalist lows of stereoscopic and gimmick horrors such as *House of Wax* (1953) (Leeder, 2011).

Overall the impression is not very edifying. Hollywood horror after the relatively high budget and highly esteemed 1930s productions falls away markedly in quality but not in quantity, as Universal and the smaller studios seemingly compete to make the most inept horrors as vehicles for faded stars. Is a nadir reached with 1948's *Abbott and Costello meet Frankenstein*? This comedy horror brings together the two comedians along with a host of the Universal monsters in their trademark makeup. The monster mashups now involving comedians continued into the 1950s and are one of the cinematic backgrounds to Hammer's own work. Both Karloff and Lugosi, doubtless pleased to get a pay cheque, were making comedy horrors by the 1950s.

Thus we should remember a point about the early development of *The Curse of Frankenstein*: it was originally going to at least partly comedic (Meikle, 2009: 37). The original intention was to make a comedic version, not a straight one, of the Frankenstein story. Few traces of this original intention show through in the finished film bar some very black humour, the comedic idea otherwise being obliterated by Cushing's very intense portrayal of the Baron and Fisher's serious handling of the material. The notion of the 1956 production being a comedy or spoof of the stories is thus confined to the footnotes of the histories written about Hammer. But it is actually an important point and is a reminder of the condition of the horror industry in both Britain and the United States prior to 1956 and to the creative intentions that prompted Hammer to put a *Frankenstein* film into production. From initial planning for a black and white comedy version of Frankenstein, all the plans, budgets and intentions changed to create a serious film.

Cushing and all the rest of the cast played the material totally straight and Fisher's stately and measured direction created a film that was far removed from any comedy. There are, as Meikle points out, some humorous lines in the script but Cushing delivers them deadpan (2009: 37). Cushing's intense and quietly spoken performance owes nothing to the broad strokes of a Bud Abbott or a Lou Costello. But in 1956, some of the most recently successful horror films were those featuring Abbott and Costello, which included not only 1948's *Abbott and Costello meet Frankenstein*, but *Abbott and Costello meet the Killer Boris Karloff* and *Abbott and Costello meet the Mummy* (1955). Once again we see an adaptive impulse at work at Hammer, even if it is one that ultimately travelled down a dead end. But in 1956, in casting about for relatively recent examples of successful horror making, the Abbott and Costello films were likely inspirations for Hammer's creative personnel to seize upon. The film historian Mark Miller dismisses the horror output immediately before *Curse* as 'shoddy, unimaginative' (1995), but as accurate as these comments might be in terms of production values or scripting, these films do have an importance in the trajectory that leads us towards *Curse*. Dixon says (1991: 223) that Abbott and Costello's 1948 film *Abbott and Costello Meet Frankenstein* left the horror genre moribund, but the commercial success of the film, its sequels and the inspiration it provided to the early development of Hammer's own film challenge this verdict.

The Abbott and Costello comedy horrors were the last hurrah for a number of Universal monsters. Bela Lugosi returned as Dracula in *Abbott and Costello meet Frankenstein* and Lon Chaney Jnr. played the Wolf Man. The verdicts that the films are shoddy or unimaginative are only a part truth. The films had coherent plots and *Meet Frankenstein* has a traditional horror narrative of attempted brain transplantation. There are also moments of genuine spookiness; *Abbott and Costello meet the Killer, Boris Karloff* was censored in some countries, including a scene of corpses playing card games.

These monster mashups were among the few examples of viable horror film production around in the 1950s. They were cheap to make and popular at the box office: *Meet Frankenstein* cost only $792,270 to make and recouped over $3 million (Furmanek & Palumbo, 1991: 175). Previous evaluations of *The Curse of Frankenstein* have tended to dismiss the original plan to have made a comedic version, but it is an important point in terms of thinking about this film as an adapting work. These comedy horrors presented to Hammer's executives a cheap but popular reconfiguration of classic monsters.

Thinking about *Curse* in this light can be liberating in terms of the weight of history than has come to rest on it and the entire Hammer company. Histories of Hammer or more broadly of the British film industry have tended to think of the company as a 'plucky' small scale British enterprise taking on larger and more threatening rivals, especially in America. Familiar parts of this narrative trajectory include Universal's initial threats and their efforts to stop the registration of the title of the film in the United States. But these views can be disingenuous. From the outset, far from being just a little British company, Hammer was backed up by American studio money and the ever-brilliant James Carreras signed profitable distribution deals with Hollywood studios. There is also an American influence at work on the early development of *The Curse of Frankenstein* as the earliest drafts, the comedic ones, were by the American film maker Milton Subotsky. While the general consensus among historians of horror cinema are that the American horrors of the 1940s and early 1050s were made to diminishing returns in terms of quality, this judgement can overlook their continuing success at the box office, especially with the drawcard of two widely popular comedians getting in on the act. Likewise, thinking of *Curse of Frankenstein* as an adapting work can make clear that in Britain in the 1950s, there was a clear antecedent for Hammer's first effort in the comedy horrors.

Ultimately *Curse* only drew on American antecedents in limited ways. As Hutchings points out, Hammer anchored their horrors in a middle European past and gave centre stage to middle aged rather than teenaged actors, in contrast to contemporary American efforts (Hutchings, 2003: 31). But in seeking answer for where *Curse* came from and the earlier successes it capitalised on, the enduring if ramshackle horrors of Universal and poverty row of the 1940s and 1950s require attention and have often been marginalised in accounts of Hammer's history. While a film such as *Abbott and Costello Meet the Mummy* is often described as a sad ending to the once respectable Universal horrors, this standard judgments overlooks the popularity of it and other films of the type (indeed Universal was still using excerpts from the film in new works as late as 1965 including *The World of Abbott and Costello*) ensured there was both a space for horror and an approach to it that makes sense of Hammer's actions in 1956.

NATIVE BRITISH HORROR

Looking to the enduring if critically disreputable efforts of Universal and poverty row in the 1940s and 1950s provides a more meaningful source of inspiration for Hammer's efforts than anything that may have been happening in Britain. If, as Pirie points out, American studios appropriated native British literature to make horror films, then in fairness it could be pointed out that British film makers were not all that interested in making such films themselves or adapting from those books. Histories of British cinema and of its horror cinema in particular make two points. One is that there are only a handful of instances of horror films (including *The Ghoul* of 1933 and *Dark Eyes of London* of 1939, with Karloff and Lugosi respectively brought over from Hollywood to star) made in Britain before *The Curse of Frankenstein* inaugurated Hammer's intensive decades of horror production. The second associated point is that the cultural and political parameters that defined British film making were hardly conducive to horror production.

For a time in the 1930s Hollywood itself shut down horror productions in the belief they were unfashionable and unprofitable. Part of this belief was fuelled by the actions of both British censors and the local municipal authorities which had authority to ban horror films from showing. County councils and the Licensing Committee did not so much view the H certificate as providing a means for horror films to be shown but rather they hoped that no films would be so dreadful to actually merit a H certificate. A few did creep through, including *The Ghoul*. Exclusive Films, which was actually the distribution arm of Hammer, distributed some horror including *The Vampire Bat*. Then in 1936 Karloff came back to Britain to make *The Man Who Changed His Mind* (known in the USA as *The Man Who Lived Again*) (Jacobs, 2011: 198). The body-swapping science fiction presented in this film was dressed up with some horror trappings. The mad scientist Dr Laurence (Karloff) conducts his experiments on brain and personality transplantation in an old dark cobwebby house and he has a deformed sidekick. The film showcases some mild body horror as well as fiendish experiments on a monkey. But *The Ghoul* and *The Man Who Changed His Mind* are oddities; largely dead ends rather than trajectories in film making. Their directors were not specialists in horror or in any way committed to the genre. *The Man Who Changed His Mind* was directed by Robert Stevenson, a versatile film maker who worked across a wide variety of styles (he later directed Mary Poppins, 1964) and whose horror film was a one off. Karloff would return to make more films in England, but later, in the 1960s, when he came back to England to make among others *The Sorcerers* (1967) for Michael Reeves and *The Curse of the Crimson Altar* (1968) for Vernon Sewell. By then, Hammer horror was in full swing and other British or Anglo-American film production companies and distributors including Amicus, Tigon, Lippert, Anglo-Amalgamated and American International Pictures were making horrors. In the 1930s however few directors or companies would make them, few cinema managers would show them, and few local authorities and municipal councils wanted there to be films requiring a H certificate.

Such attitudes endured. They endured in the willingness of local authorities to flatly ban H films (and later X films) and in the attitudes of censors and critics who were bewildered and angry that film makers continued to make such sickening products. The point of the H certificate was to discourage horror films. In the 1930s at least the discouragement seems to have worked, mostly. Besides *The Ghoul* and *Dark Eyes of London* (which earned a H certificate) British film makers mostly eschewed the horrific and supernatural, and Hollywood horrors were often outright banned, including 1932's *Freaks* by Tod Browning. The director of Hollywood's Production Code Administration (and many Universal horrors were 'pre-code') assured the BBFC that Hollywood did not wish to offend British sensibilities (Johnson, 1997: 145).

But by the 1950s critics were concerned the fight seemed to be slipping away. Earlier we encountered Derek Hill's splenetic review of Hammer films in *Sight and Sound* in 1958. From the same piece comes this plaintive lament that 'the displays, the posters and the slogans have become an accepted part of the West End scene. So too, have the queues. The horror boom […] is still prospering. Why?' (cited in Cooper, 2011: 31). It clearly did not occur to him that writing a piece promoting films as being so excitingly lurid as containing sights fit for the concentration camps might actually have inadvertently promoted the horror boom. There is an important point lurking in Hill's overreaction: he points out that horror films were becoming an established part of the landscape, literally so in terms of the billboards and posters, but also as a routine part of what cinemas were showing. A year before *Curse* went into production at Bray Abbott and Costello had released their comedy-horror mummy film. William Castle's gimmick horrors, as well as pulp American horrors such as *The Fly* were in production or soon would be. The horror genre in Britain gives the impression of lying dormant but ready for activation.

CONCLUSION

We are now at a point to see several contrasting traditions and factors at play. Even if the British film industry had proved reluctant to adapt it, British literature had produced a volume of gothic texts that Hollywood had found to be a viable source of adaptation. While conventional wisdom insists that these horrors made in Hollywood by Universal eventually tailed off in quality, they did not lose popularity, giving Hammer a viable model for adaptation. But other cinematic influences came into play as Fisher's background at Gainsborough, the nascent British horror industry and Hammer itself all converge at a particular moment in time when Fisher, Cushing and the rest of the Hammer team all assembled in Black Park, erected the gibbet, and began shooting the very first scenes of *Curse of Frankenstein*.

FOOTNOTES

6.   Dixon made this point to me in an email.

CHAPTER FIVE: CINEMA PART 2: HERITAGE AND HORROR

In *The Curse of Frankenstein* the Baron conducts his diabolical experiments among circumstances of considerable charm and comfort, almost akin to an 'upstairs/downstairs' juxtaposition of adjoining but contrasting worlds popular from period dramas such as *Downton Abbey* or the original *Upstairs Downstairs* itself. Fisher creates what Hutchings calls a 'solid, thoroughly materialistic world' (Hutchings, 1996: 117). Frankenstein's bio-mechanical experiments on dead tissue and organs are carried out in the same house where he lives his ostensibly respectable life with his fiancée Elizabeth. Eventually the façade cracks and then shatters in the most embarrassing of ways; Elizabeth and the authorities discover the Baron's scientific depravity, the monster erupts into view, and the Baron is dragged off to the local prison and kept among the common prisoners prior to being taken to the guillotine. By the end of the film the dandified Baron is a grubby, sweaty man in shabby clothes, far removed from the poised and elegant figure he cut in his chateau. The gold fob watch, top hat, cane and cloak have gone.

Elegance lost as the Baron is imprisoned

The Curse of Frankenstein is a hybrid, adapting from a novel but by no means suggesting that the film is subordinate to the literature. Nor is it committed to the realistic. The film instead sits in the trajectory established by Gainsborough period dramas, which the 'upstairs/downstairs' aesthetic of the Baron's world indicates. *Curse*'s extremely stately opening even gives the impression of being another period 'bodice ripper' as Fisher holds back on anything horrific happening until way into the film's running time. This point indicates an important aspect this chapter explores of where *Curse of Frankenstein* came from and why it was so shocking, as critics saw the sumptuous period trappings of costume drama turned to the altogether darker and more gruesome ends of the horror film.

Hitherto the continuities in personnel and style between the small Gainsborough operation and the equally close knit work at Bray has been noted but not explored in depth in terms of their creative implications. In particular the adaptation from the themes and style of the Gainsborough melodramas is an explanation for a major aspect of the transgression from the book made by the film and in the way the central character of the Baron was written, framed and made to interact with the supporting characters.

DIRECTING HORROR: FISHER BEFORE HAMMER

Horror film making in Britain was, as we saw in the previous chapter, extremely limited prior to Hammer's experiment with *The Curse of Frankenstein*. Whatever limited horror production there had been in Britain before *Curse* had not involved Terence Fisher. His career is a peculiar one. Fisher is now thought of as a horror specialist, but seen in broader perspective his career is bifurcated in a way that indicates the restrictions on horror that prevailed in the British film industry. The general indifference from critics or obituary writers at his death in 1980 has been made up for since by an extensive body of critical writings, including biographies and filmographies. But what has been written about him tends to focus almost exclusively on his Hammer films (as well as the works he completed in the 1960s for small studios on the occasions when Hammer was employing other directors, including his science fiction thrillers *The Earth Dies Screaming* and *Night of the Big Heat*, both cheap films for small studios). The decade he spent directing an eclectic range of films before beginning work on *Curse of Frankenstein* languishes in the shadows of his Hammer work, because Fisher is evaluated as a horror specialist. Film historians have found it hard to make the early films fit into the contours of his later career.

However some aspects of his career do present themselves as significant to understanding not only how he came to direct *Curse*, but also the type of film and the nature of the adaptation which he shaped. Even though Fisher was not making horror films prior to 1956, he was a busy director, including making crime dramas and costume dramas. The confluence of circumstances that put Fisher in that right place and at that right time have been well enough accounted for in biographies by Dixon and Hutchings to not need restatement. However a few aspects of what he was up to before 1956 and his convergence with Cushing, Lee and Carreras at Bray stand out as important.

The main details of Fisher's life have been told effectively by Hutchings and particularly by Dixon, who was fortunate to access interviews with Fisher from before his death in 1980 and who was able to interview Fisher's widow in person. Having been the oldest clapper boy around, starting in that lowly capacity at the Limegrove studios in 1933 at the age of 29 (Dixon, 1991: 6), Fisher rapidly rose from position of third assistant director to second assistant director to assistant editor in 1934 (Dixon, 1991: 7). He became a much-sought after editor, sometimes working on up to ten films a year. By 1948 Fisher was handed his first directing project, the modest 60 minute B feature *Colonel Bogey*.

Fisher made this little film for the Rank Organisation, which he had recently joined. This point is of capital significance to understanding where Fisher came from by the time we reach 1956 and his preparations for *Curse*. Lord Rank's sprawling movie empire, whose films were marked out by the famous gong and gong beater of the Rank ident, encompassed a number of nominally distinct film making entities, including Highbury studios and Gainsborough studios. The latter of these had its own distinctive ident of a lady in eighteenth-century costume sitting inside an ornate picture frame, in emulation of the company's namesake, the eighteenth-century portraitist and landscape artist Thomas Gainsborough (Cook, 2009: 254).

These disparate groups were presided over by J. Arthur Rank, a teetotal Methodist. Lord Rank would not have entertained the idea of making a disreputable gothic horror film and indeed the projects Fisher helmed for the Rank Organisation are far removed from the later horrors that his name is now synonymous with. Despite this disjunction, some of Fisher's biographers have attempted to locate thematic consistency or coherence in Fisher's pre-horror directing projects. Pirie for example attempted to distil what he regarded as characteristic Fisherian themes and preoccupations from the director's pre-1956 projects, such as a preoccupation with external deceit hiding inner decay, as well as a distinct xenophobia. Also attempting to pinpoint a consistency in Fisher's career by suggesting he was making horror films before anyone realised it, including Fisher himself, Pirie suggests that one of Fisher's Gainsborough/Rank projects, *So Long at the Fair* (1950) could 'easily have been re-shot, sequence for sequence, as a vampire movie without making any difference to its basic mechanics, for the same dualistic structure pervades every frame' (Pirie, 1981).

However, there are several problems with these efforts to account for the sudden emergence of Fisher in 1956 as a gothic horror specialist by attempting to project consistencey back into his career. One, as Dixon has pointed out, is that Pirie's assertions were based on limited evidence, as so few of Fisher's pre-1956 films were available for viewing when Pirie was writing in the early 1970s (Dixon: 116). Another is that when Fisher's surviving films from before 1956 actually are examined, they reveal an extraordinary eclecticism in tone, themes and subject matter, not to mention quality, that any attempts to pinpoint a distinctive if nascent 'Fisherian' set of tropes or preoccupations becomes problematic.

Yet we should not dismiss entirely the idea of a series of formative influences at work on Fisher and the adaptation of Frankenstein. He did after all burst forth seemingly fully formed as a horror director in 1956, but his work on *Curse of Frankenstein* did not emerge from a vacuum. Even if Fisher's career lacked any particular consistency, we can nonetheless reconstruct some points of importance. These include the trajectory of Fisher's career, which took him closer and closer to Hammer, to Bray and to the production personnel working there, as well as the types of projects he seems to have valued as a journeyman, as opposed to those where he very clearly just pointed the camera, shot the film, and went home.

FISHER THE DIRECTOR

The Curse of Frankenstein is stately but it is certainly not slow and the action rattles briskly through the 80 minutes running time. To create balance and structure, Fisher puts the film together largely as a sequence of medium shots, carefully composed and balanced, from which he sometimes cuts away to a close-up. His directing style and use of cameras are discussed in depth by Dixon. The film is inevitably quite static, as much of the running time comprises master shots of two people in the frame talking to each other. The visual style of Fisher's major films for Gainsborough such as *So Long at the Fair* carry over into his first gothic horror. From the beginning of *Curse* Fisher sets up a series of mostly static shots which are framed by a doorway. At the beginning it is the priest entering the prison. Many shots are of two people, mostly Frankenstein and Krempe, framed by the double doors of the drawing room or the door of the laboratory, acting before a static camera. Fisher does however break these up with expressive close-ups and cutaways, such as Krempe attempting to calm the frighten horse at the gibbet when the corpse drops. Fisher intercuts this close-up into a wide shot of the area around the gibbet. Krempe is shown looking perturbed in another close-up in a medium master shot when the Baron is cutting the dead criminal's head off.

But Fisher achieves a great deal within these static shots and assessments of his directing style have often pointed out his ability to stage dynamic action in front of an almost stationary camera. Normally the scene signalled out as illustrative of this ability is the moment in *Horror of Dracula* when Lee's character appears coming down stairs, and swoops dynamically into shot while the camera stays put. But similar dynamism had been achieved in *Curse of Frankenstein*. Fisher's camera stays still in scenes including the fight between the Baron and Krempe in the vault and later when the creature awakes and begins to viciously throttle Frankenstein and the scenes come to life without the camera needing to move around the actors. Fisher achieves a great deal within these carefully composed shots. One of the blackest and most sardonically amusing moments in the film comes when the Baron has invited the Professor to dinner, ostensibly for a brief overnight stay but in reality to murder him and steal his brain. As Elizabeth innocently says that the Professor has 'the greatest brain in Europe', Victor turns to the Professor sitting next to him and glances briefly and speculatively at his head. The moment comes and goes in the blink of an eye. The shot is immaculately set and framed, with Victor and the Professor sitting side by side on a sofa, smoking cigars and drinking brandy, all framed in midshot. A close up on Victor as he turned to appraise the

Eyeing up the greatest brain in Europe

Professor's head would have been crude and would have unsubtly rammed home a point about the Baron's character. Instead Fisher achieves a more subtle point with a brief midshot and Cushing accomplishes the same with his acting. This framing and editing allows Fisher and Cushing together to achieve this moment of dark humour and character development.

Earlier on I quoted John Carpenter's appreciative observation of Fisher's choreographed scenes of mayhem and the comment nearly captures the essence of Fisher's visual style. Neat framings and coherent action define his films. The efforts of some historians and critics to adduce the defining 'fisherian' characteristics may neglect that his films before 1956 are widely eclectic in narrative, themes, style and even just in Fisher's imaginative and technical approach to the material. But there is an important prelude to his Hammer films and to the dignified and stately horror scenes he staged: his work for Gainsborough.

POINTS OF ORIGIN: SCIENCE FICTION OR COSTUME HORROR?

Gainsborough studios may on first evidence be a strange place to look for insights about the production and reception of *Curse*. It was part of the god-fearing Lord Rank's empire and produced films in a variety of popular genres, including Will Hay comedies and the costume dramas starring the likes of Margaret Lockwood, James Mason and Stewart Granger. Because it seems an unlikely place to look for Fisher's grisly mayhem, historians' and commentators' attention has normally been directed to a different point of origin for Hammer's horror output in the Quatermass films of 1955 onwards. The Quatermass films are far removed from the sumptuous period design and Victorian-era scientific apparatus in *Curse*. They were set in the (for the 1950s) present day and with narratives involving alien invasion. They were, like so much else made by Hammer, adaptations, in this case from two BBC drama productions written by Nigel Kneale and produced by Rudolph Cartier.[7] Most often historians of the Hammer company suggest that *Curse of Frankenstein* went into production after the company experienced major success with its *Quatermass* films and *X the Unknown* and elected to make *another* horror film.

However this oft-repeated narrative neglects the fact that the *Quatermass* films are science fiction with contemporary British settings, not gothic horrors set in an indeterminate nineteenth-century Europe. There is little in these films' tone, style or sources to account for the company's decision to make a Frankenstein film. There is more to splitting hairs over genre in this point: moving away from the supposed influence of *Quatermass* allows for the foundation of this major strand of British and horror movie making to be understood in new ways.

While historians of Hammer films tend to locate the Quatermass serials and *X the Unknown* as the 'Ur texts', or origin texts, of the company's successful horror cycles, this view can be adjusted. Certainly the films showed Hammer's executives that there was a profitable market to be had from X rated material. The films also consolidated Hammer's already winning formula of adapting from the BBC that had begun with the Dick Barton films, continued with Terence Fisher's *Spaceways* and now continued with Nigel Kneale's science fiction scripts (although *X the Unknown* was an original story by Jim Sangster, it was meant to include the character of Professor Quatermass). But in other important respects these science fiction thrillers of the mid 1950s are false starts or even dead ends. They are contemporary rather than period or costume dramas. *The Quatermass Xperiment* very clearly located menace in everyday reality, including the famous climax in Westminster Abbey, a location recently seen by the then largest yet television viewing audience at the coronation of Queen Elizabeth II (Harmes,

2013: 220). The second Quatermass film likewise juxtaposed the alien threat with the drab modernity of prefab huts and factories. The science fiction films are scientifically rational (even if the science is of the outer space variety) rather than supernatural. The key difference then is that they are not gothic. They are not distillations of the dark, hidden and grotesque world that *Curse* would promote, nor are they attempts to create an indeterminate European 'other' in a British film studio, such as Gainsborough's melodrama *Madonna of the Seven Moons* (1944).

Science fiction ultimately is a road that Hammer did not travel and *Curse* killed off the black and white thrillers the studio was producing (Miller, 1995: 69). Whatever science fiction was made in Britain in the late-1950s and 1960s emerged from other studios. There are a number of such films from the noteworthy and successful such as *Village of the Damned* (1960) and *The Day the Earth Caught Fire* (1964) to more light-hearted fare such as *The Trygon Factor* (1967) to the simply bizarre *Zeta One* (1969). But these were not Hammer efforts. Even Fisher's science fiction thrillers were made for other studios. Although the company's creative personnel were omnivorous adapters from of course gothic texts but also swashbucklers and pirate stories (such as Russell Thorndyke's books), from 'ripping yarns' in the mould of G.A. Henty with films like *Stranglers of Bombay* and from successful television sitcoms, science fiction was not a repeating pattern. Hammer's own audience research showed that audiences wanted horror, not science fiction (Dixon, 1991: 224).

A number of important parallels between another studio and Hammer direct attention away from science fiction to Gainsborough. While part of a larger film empire, Gainsborough was a small-scale operation with a repertory of performers and technicians. The Gainsborough networks that later formed at Bray were extensive, encompassing not only Fisher and Asher and Len Harris the camera operator, but also the crucial figure of Anthony Nelson-Keys, the producer (Dixon, 1991: 227). The name of the company is synonymous with a particular type of output, namely costume melodrama, based on the more fantastical and gothic elements inherent in British storytelling, a trajectory that also includes Hammer (Cook, 1996b: 54). The company's costume dramas also gained their dramatic impulse from the deliberate archaisms and period details, an impulse that recurs in Baron Frankenstein's laboratory.

Gainsborough's output was popular at the book office but also often critically derided at the time of release and has since been mostly neglected by film scholars, although a small number of historians including Pam Cook have attempted the recuperation of the company's reputation (Petrie, 1997: 118). Any attempt to recuperate or champion this studio has required the assertion of the validity of a non-realistic aesthetic in British cinema. As Petrie points out, from the 1950s onwards many critics and many film makers championed a 'documentary-realistic aesthetic' as a major hallmark of British cinema (127-128). A studio-bound, anti-realist set of film aesthetics would inevitably incur disdain in comparison and have only a low cultural status in the eyes of critics who privileged what Cook calls the 'austere realism' of post-war cinema (Cook, 1996b: 53). Gainsborough established and then swiftly consolidated its reputation as a breeding ground for actors, technicians and directors unhappy at working within the realist orthodoxy (Harper, 1994: 119). The Gainsborough costume cycle was comparatively short-lived, lasting from 1943's *The Man in Grey* to 1950's *So Long at the Fair* (co-directed by Terence Fisher); but while short lived the cycle comprised popular and attention grabbing films made by a close-knit team. *So Long at the Fair* was a breakaway from the B features that Fisher had mostly been doing. It had a reasonable budget and a prestige cast including Dirk Bogarde, Jean Simmons, David Tomlinson and Honor Blackman. Its period setting (it is about the mysterious disappearance by a young man at the 1889 Exposition Universelle) and its sumptuous trappings, not to mention its highly sinister atmosphere, make clear why is seems so strongly a precursor to Fisher's Hammer work.

What is often neglected in assessments of Hammer and their inaugural gothic film is the heritage of transgression that follows a transit from Gainsborough into Hammer. In Hammer, exaggerated and amplified by the gore and violence brought into the narrative by the horror trappings, these transgressive elements took on new life. Some film historians have noted the trajectories of careers from Gainsborough to Hammer that made this new life possible. Petrie points out that what he calls the 'Hammer aesthetic' of colour film, period sets and costume are aspects exported out of Gainsborough along with key technical personnel including Fisher, Harris and Asher (1997: 135). It is also of course anti-realist and non-documentary in style. The lavish and non-realistic sets and costumes reflect the sumptuousness that typified a Gainsborough picture; former

Gainsborough alumnus Anthony Nelson-Keys was particularly proud of the costume and set design on *Curse* (Dixon, 1991: 227).

CRITICAL REACTIONS

The Gainsborough melodramas attracted a critical press as emotive as the barbs against Hammer's films. Comments such as 'nauseating' were routinely applied to the films, as were criticisms that the historical dramas were unfaithful to the sources. *The Wicked Lady*, set during the reign of King Charles II (1660-1685), attracted criticism for multiple historical inaccuracies (Cook, 1996: 64-65). The critical opprobrium given to the Gainsborough films were a prelude to the similar comments made about *Curse*. Back in chapter one I also compared the critical reaction to *Curse* to the vitriol three years later about Michael Powell's *Peeping Tom* of 1960. The comparisons are not absolute. The Gainsborough films were period features like *Curse*, but were not horror films. *Curse* was a horror film, as was *Peeping Tom*, but *Peeping Tom* was set in the present day and was not a gothic horror.

This last contrast is important to understand the reactions to Hammer's film. *Curse* and *Peeping Tom* had almost identical critical reactions (the films were disgusting, debasing, cinema had stooped to an indefensible low, the people who made them were sick) but contrasting outcomes. Fisher's film made his career; Powell's ended his. These differences feed back into the nature of the films. Even if critics felt that Hammer's film was disgusting, its horrors were safely back in an indeterminate, European past. Powell by contrast had brought his horrors much too close to home. The film was set in present day London and its queasy and uneasy plot of a young film technician murdering women was made all the more direct and confronting by Powell's narrative showing the origin of the man's perversions in his troubled childhood and by Powell casting his own son in the role of the disturbed little boy. The horrors in this way were immediate and in the present.

PERIOD HORROR

Although the year that *Curse* is set in is indeterminate it is at least 150 years earlier than 1956 and the action is remote where Powell's was contemporary. Throughout the film Fisher reinforces the juxtaposition of the respectable and the immoral that the period setting promotes. Towards the beginning of the film he dissolves from a scene of Frankenstein and Krempe relaxing in their drawing room and chinking their brandy glasses together to one of their arrival at the gibbet where the dead robber is hanging. In a later scene in the drawing room Elizabeth rhapsodises about her and Victor's mutual love and Fisher cuts immediately to Frankenstein groping Justine. Later in the film Fisher cuts from a scene of Frankenstein fastidiously pulling on his surgical gloves prior to performing brain surgery to him coming downstairs in impeccable evening dress, adjusting his cuffs with the same fastidiousness. Frankenstein's action – moving downstairs into civilisation away from the charnel house of his laboratory upstairs – reinforces the differences between the worlds, but the same level of sartorial fastidiousness indicates that he belongs to both the respectable and the infernal domains that he inhabits.

The actor bringing the Baron to life, Peter Cushing, felt at home among the period trappings the Hammer set designers created at Bray. Cushing himself was an aficionado of history and historical artefacts, as the recollections of his co-stars and colleagues testify (Eddington, 1995: 114-115). In daily life and in interviews he even dressed in historically inflected clothing, including an appearance on Terry Wogan's chat show in 1987 dressed in a nineteenth-century style suit that he had been given by the BBC when he was playing Sherlock Holmes. By 1957 he was already used to appearing in costume drama, having been in Laurence Olivier's lavish period dress adaptation of *Hamlet* (1948), BBC Shakespeare adaptations, as well as playing Mr Darcy in the BBC's 1952 adaptation of Jane Austen's *Pride and Prejudice*. Besides the addition of the monster, the gibbet and the laboratory apparatus, Cushing would have felt right at home among the period trappings at Bray.

But because Hammer adapted not just from Shelley and not just from Universal, but also from the Gainsborough melodramas that reliable old hands like Fisher and Asher had worked on, their horrors were altogether more remote because of these period trappings. Nor were they taken entirely seriously; although the most frequently quoted reviews from 1957 about *Curse* are the ones which expressed horror at the moral corruption engendered by the film, others were more lightly mocking (Hutchings). They share this tone with the reviews which ridiculed Gainsborough for getting their history of King Charles II muddled up.

ARISTOCRACY AND ADAPTATION

Although the continuities in personnel between Gainsborough and Hammer have been noted by historians of both companies, as has the basic point that Hammer was making costume dramas in the Gainsborough mould, these points deserve to be stretched further. Particularly so in terms of the how the original Frankenstein story was adapted into Hammer's first gothic horror. More than just personnel and costume carried over from one studio to another; so too did important dimensions of the adaptation of sources into films.

One of them is the treatment of the aristocracy. Throughout *Curse*'s running time the audience is constantly reminded of Frankenstein's aristocratic status, one missing from Shelley's book (see chapter three). In the early scenes of his childhood he is already precociously arrogant, bullying his relatives and peremptorily interviewing his new tutor, Krempe. The adult character played by Cushing is in Pirie's words 'a magnificently arrogant aristocratic rebel' who lives comfortably with access to women, wine and cigars (Pirie 1981). Curiously this aspect of the character would become more and more diluted as the Hammer Frankenstein series continued and the Baron became more and more bourgeois, living in humdrum surroundings (a doctor's surgery in *Frankenstein Created Woman*, a guest house in *Frankenstein Must be Destroyed*, an asylum in *Frankenstein and the Monster from Hell*) and looking less and less like the Byronic dandy of the first film. But in *Curse*, the central character is firmly located in a louche aristocratic milieu. Cushing's Baron flaunts his aristocratic status; he toys with his gold fobwatch, goes out and about in a top cane, cloak and with a cane and bullies servants and family.

The dramatic potential of wicked aristocracy is adapted from Gainsborough, as is the locating of this aristocracy in a generic historical milieu. Gainsborough's costume cycle came to an end when new management changed the studio's focus based on the belief that audiences wanted to see films set in the present day (Harper, 1994: 121). By the early 1950s the costume cycle was at an end, but Hammer's executives had meanwhile poached technicians and producers from Gainsborough in the belief that audiences still wanted costume films. Admittedly Gainsborough did not have a monopoly on period-set drama involving the bourgeoisie and higher echelons. Crime films set in the past ranged from *Uncle Silas* (1947, an adaptation from J. Sheridan le Fanu), *The Mark of Cain* (1948) and *Madeleine* (1950) (Gillett, 2003: 133). These films, especially the first, do though inhabit a similar world which emphasises the wickedness of the rich. They also invoke the emphasis on a lush period setting as a background to sexual tension and drama that is anti-realist in its aesthetic (Collins, 2012). These were costume films centred on the crimes of the aristocracy.

Study of particular iterations of aristocratic villainy in the Gainsborough films indicate that the source novels were adapted in a way to reinforce or even freshly create this aspect of the plots, a creative process that strikingly parallels what Jimmy Sangster did to Shelley's novel. The adaptation of the novel *Caravan* turned what Harper calls an 'amiable invalid' into the outrageous villain Sir Francis, of whom in the film a whore said 'he's a beast, he's the worst of the lot' (Harper, 1996: 125). The honest aristocratic character in the novel *The Man in Grey* became in the film adaptation what Harper (ibid.) calls 'a Byronic misogynist'. In all, deliberate adaptive transgressions created aristocratic characters in films that were 'the site of fascination, fear, and unspeakable dark sexuality' (Harper, 1996: 126).

The parallel with what happened to the republican son of a Swiss syndic in Shelley's novel to the character that Sangster created and Cushing embodied is striking. One commentator characterises Cushing's Baron as a 'charming yet corrupt dandy' (Newman, 2011), and the performance and the way the role is written traces an ancestry back to the wicked aristocrats of the Gainsborough bodice rippers, not to Shelley's novel. The character in the film sexually exploited his maid servant, and more generally exploited friends, family and colleagues. Particular messages about aristocratic power are conveyed by the writing, acting and production in *Curse*, from the very fact that Sangster made Frankenstein a Baron to the ornate interior design of the chateau. The treatment of the aristocracy in Fisher's films has been subject to contrasting critical assessment, including claims that they are distinctly anti-aristocratic in sentiment, a point evaluated by Hutchings in his biography of Fisher (2001: 100-101). Regardless of where

Fisher's or the company's sympathies may have lain, the film does certainly exploit the potential for wicked aristocracy. So far we have heard that critics objected to perceived violence and gore in the Hammer films, but the dark, sexualised aristocracy of the film and the earlier Gainsborough costume cycles is an overlooked aspect of what worried critics so much. The very fact that *Curse* is set in an indeterminate historical period both allowed Hammer to foreground the aristocratic villainy of the central character but also meant the film was including aspects which had traditionally worried the British Board of Film Censors. Although the Baron was shown amidst a background of ornate period trappings, the dandified evil of the role remained a current and ongoing preoccupation with both cinema patrons and censors. The ruthlessness of the character was as contemporary as other cinematic and literary sensations of the period from *Room at the Top* to the James Bond novels (Newman, 2011). But the portrayal of a corrupt aristocracy was especially worrying.

The portrayal of the aristocracy on film was also current. The Board of Film Censors had long frowned upon more than just horrific content; films with working class characters were also unpopular, such as the Old Mother Riley films, and conversely the Board was also worried about offending the sensibilities of the aristocracy (Harper, 1994: 151). But by the post-war period the number of films being made with historical settings was growing, and historical settings allowed for the portrayal of a lurid and louche aristocracy. To an extent, the executives at Gainsborough were determined to have their cake and eat it; their films were as risqué as was possible in that era, and the company's output was designed for mass appeal. But the company also played the quality card, positioning their films within a discourse of art and culture (Cook, 2009: 254). A similar strategy did not emerge from Hammer, although the industry professionals making *Curse* were themselves upholding the highest standards based on their many years of experience. But no similar claims for quality emerged from Hammer, whose executives were content to unleash the violence.

The Gainsborough films which showcased this decadent aristocracy deviated markedly from the source novels, as did Sangster. For this reason Cook is right to judge the costume dramas as hybrids, incorporating sources of inspiration and ideas from literature but also from other forms and types of storytelling (Cook, 1996b: 58). If we scrape away the accumulations that have accreted on *Curse* we get a similar sense of its powerful hybridity. It is a film that made daring use of Shelley's novel, that plundered from disparate strands of Hollywood and British horror and which did unspeakable things to the costume drama genre. These are points from which the film emerged, not narratives of its later influence. Mary Shelley, daughter of William Godwin and Mary Wollstonecraft, reader of Milton, admirer of Swiss republicanism, may well have been surprised by the dandy at the heart of the story as told by Sangster and directed by Fisher, although there were the echoes of her friend Lord Byron. The dandified Baron traces his ancestry to a source beyond the novel to another type of storytelling and from a team that started out at Gainsborough but who brought their ideas on decadent aristocracy across to Bray.

Footnotes

7. There had been a third BBC serial chronicling Professor Quatermass's adventures, 1958/1959's *Quatermass and the Pit*. Hammer did not get around to making an adaptation until 1967.

CONCLUSION

A great deal of detritus clings to *The Curse of Frankenstein*. This detritus makes it seem the foundation for a long-running formula for over twenty years' worth of gothic horror production. If seen in these terms, the freshness, vitality and innovation of the film all collapse under the weight of later history. More ominously, the standard histories of the Hammer studio note that the many gothic films that came in *Curse*'s wake eventually fell into a downward trajectory, becoming stale, cheaply exploitative, or rather sexploitative, derivative and commercially unpopular. *Curse* is thus not only regarded as the beginning of a tradition, but a tradition that outstayed its welcome.

My goal has been to sift through these perceptions, placing emphasis on the film as an adaptation of multiple sources, all brought into dialogue with each other. While there are a few fundamental components from Shelley's novel included in the film, the script by Sangster and the production by Fisher created cinematic solutions for a book that was essentially incapable of 'faithful' adaptation. The very inspiration for Hammer to make a horror film came from works most often relegated to the footnotes of horror history, the comedy horrors of the 1940s and 1950s. The film's style and tone, and the working ethos of a small close-knit team, moved across from Gainsborough to Bray.

Critical reactions to the film from reviewers in the national and trade press have often been quoted in histories of Hammer and the general consensus is that critics hated the film but it succeeded at the box office despite this critical mauling. This success was not necessarily a foregone conclusion and bad reviews could bury films and destroy directors' careers. But it is illuminating to think about what people said about the film on its release, the way it succeeded commercially and the fact it is an adaptation. Adaptation brings familiarity onto the screen in terms of what audiences may already read or seen. Adaptation can create pathways for understanding and the repetition of familiar stories or themes provides an anchor for audiences. The grace and poise of Cushing's Baron and his surroundings are one such anchor, appropriated from the earlier successful period dramas made by Gainsborough.

But using this sophisticated milieu in a horror film was both an adaptation and a transgression. The Baron throughout the film is a man pushing boundaries of class (his affair with a mere servant), morality (his murdering and tomb robbing) and science (his breakthroughs in the preservation and creation of life). The team behind the cameras pushed against barriers of their own; against a tight schedule that needed to be longer, against all prevailing trends in British cinema and in Hollywood as well, where horror had fallen from any position of studio respectability it may have had, and against critical opinion. When Cushing's Frankenstein argues with Krempe that they 'have opened the door' and must go through it, the sentiments could also be those of Fisher and his crew, arguing with Carreras for more time and for a colour feature and thereby creating a film that appalled contemporary sensibilities. With his aristocratic disdain, the Baron certainly wouldn't have cared. He created life, and likewise the energy and impact of *The Curse of Frankenstein* is a moment of genesis for horror cinema.

BIBLIOGRAPHY

Ashworth, Mark, 'Steele, Barbara', in Kim Newman (ed), *The BFI Companion to Horror*. London: Cassell, 1996, pp.301-302.

Bonner, Frances and Jacobs, Jason, 'The First Encounter: Observations on the Chronology of Encounter with some Adaptations of Lewis Carroll's Alice books', *Convergence: The International Journal of Research into New Media Technologies*, vol.17, no.1, 2011, pp.37-48.

Bright, Morris and Ross, Robert, *Fawlty Towers: Fully Booked*. London: BBC Worldwide, 2001.

Brooker, Peter, 'Postmodern Adaptation: Pastiche, Intertextuality, and Re-Functioning', in *The Cambridge Companion to Literature on Screen*, edited by Deborah Cartmell and Imelda Whelehan, Cambridge: Cambridge University Press, 2007, pp. 107-120.

Brottman, Mikita, 'B Movies and Trash', *Cult Films Film Reference*, http://www.filmreference.com/encyclopedia/Criticism-Ideology/Cult-Films-B-MOVIES-AND-TRASH.html

Brown, Simon, 'The British Silent Horror Film and the First World War', *Off Screen*, vol.14, iss.10, 2013, http://www.offscreen.com/index.php./pages/essays/british_silent_horror/

Carney, Jessica, *Who's There: The Life and Career of William Hartnell*, London: Fantom Publishing, 2013.

Cartmell, Deborah and Whelehan, Imelda (eds), *The Cambridge Companion to Literature on Screen*, Cambridge: Cambridge University Press, 2007

Chibnall, Steve and Petley, Julian (eds), *British Horror Cinema*, London: Routledge, 2002.

Collins, Frank. 'British Cult Classics: The Curse of Frankenstein', *Cathode Ray Tube*, October 2012, http://www.cathoderaytube.co.uk/2012/10/british-cult-classics-curse-of.html

Cook, Pam, *Fashioning the Nation: Costume and Identity in British Cinema*, London: British Film Institute, 1996a.

_____ (ed), *Gainsborough Pictures*, London: Cassell, 1997.

_____, 'On Memorialising Gainsborough Studios', *Journal of British Cinema and Television*, vol.6, 2009, pp.249-255.

_____, 'Neither Here nor There: National Identity in Gainsborough Costume Drama', in Andrew Higson (ed), *Dissolving Views: Key Articles on British Cinema*, London: Cassell, 1996b.

Cooper, Ian, *Devil's Advocates: Witchfinder General*. Leighton Buzzard: Auteur, 2011.

Crane, Jonathan Lake, *Terror and Everyday Life: Singular Moments in the History of the Horror Film*, Thousand Oaks: Sage, 1994.

Davies, Anthony, *Filming Shakespeare's Plays*, Cambridge: Cambridge University Press, 1988.

Dixon, Wheeler Winston, *The Charm of Evil: The Life and Films of Terence Fisher*, Metuchen, NJ: The Scarecrow Press, 1991.

Eddington, Paul, *So Far, So Good: The Autobiography*, London: Hodder and Stoughton, 1995.

Edwards, Kyle Dawson, 'Brand Name Literature: Film Adaptation and Selznick International Pictures' *Rebecca* (1940)', *Cinema Journal* 45, no.3, 2006, pp.32-58.

Forry, Steven Earl, *Hideous Progenies: Dramatizations of 'Frankenstein' from Mary Shelley to the Present*, Philadelphia: University of Pennsylvania Press, 1990.

Fox, Killian, 'Peeping Tom': No 10 best horror film of all time', *The Guardian*, 22 October, 2010, http://www.theguardian.com/film/movie/36228/peeping-tom

Furmanek, Bob and Palumbo, Ron, *Abbott and Costello in Hollywood*, New York: Perigee Books, 1991.

Gillett, Philip, *The British Working Class in Postwar Film*, Manchester: Manchester University Press, 2003.

Gritten, David. 'Michael Powell's "Peeping Tom": the film that killed a career', *The Telegraph* 27 August, 2010, http://www.telegraph.co.uk/culture/film/7967407/Michael-Powells-Peeping-Tom-the-film-that-killed-a-career.html

Hamilton, John, *The British Independent Horror Film 1951-70*, Hemlock Books, 2013.

Hand, Richard J and McRoy, Jay (eds), *Monstrous Adaptations: Generic and Thematic Mutations in Horror Film*, Manchester: Manchester University Press, 2007.

Hand, Richard J, 'Paradigms of metamorphosis and transmutation: Thomas Edison's *Frankenstein* and John Barrymore's *Dr Jekyll and Mr Hyde*' in Richard J Hand and Jay McRoy (eds), *Monstrous Adaptations: Generic and Thematic Mutations in Horror Film*, Manchester: Manchester University Press, 2007, pp.9-19.

Harmes, Marcus, 'Martians, demons, vampires and vicars: the Church of England in post-war science fiction', *The Journal of Religion and Popular Culture*, vol.25, no.2, 2013, pp.217-229.

_____, 'Why does your church look like a fortress? God and the Gothic in *Doctor Who* and Hammer', *Science Fiction Film and Television*, vol.7, no.1, 2014, pp.99-116.

Harper, Sue, *Picturing the Past: The Rise and Fall of the British Costume Film*. London: British Film Institute, 1994.

Hearn, Marcus, *The Hammer Vault*, London: Titan Books, 2011.

Heffernan, James AW, 'Looking at the Monster: *Frankenstein* and Film', *Critical Inquiry*, vol.24, no.1, 1997, pp.133-58.

Higson, Andrew (ed), *Dissolving Views: Key Articles on British Cinema*, London: Cassell, 1996.

Hogg, Thomas Jefferson, *The Life of Percy Bysshe Shelley*, London: E. Moxon, 1858.

Hunter, I.Q., *British Trash Cinema*, London: British Film Institute, 2013.

_____, 'Hang On a Minute Lads, I Got a Great Idea: Three Ways (Not) to Remake a British Cult Film', paper at *Rewriting, Remixing and Reloading: Adaptations Across the Globe*, International Conference, Centre for British Studies, Berlin, 30 September 2010.

Hutcheon, Linda, *A Theory of Adaptation*, London: Routledge, 2006.

Hutchings, Peter, *Dracula*, London: I.B. Tauris/British Film Institute, 2003.

_____, 'Fisher, Terence', in Kim Newman (ed), *The BFI Companion to Horror.* London: Cassell, 1996, p.117.

_____, *Hammer and Beyond: the British Horror Film*, Manchester: Manchester University Press, 1993.

_____, *The Horror Film*, Harlow: Pearson, 2004.

_____, *Terence Fisher*, Manchester: Manchester University Press, 2001.

Hutchinson, Tom. 'Cushing, Peter' in Kim Newman (ed), *The BFI Companion to Horror*. London: Cassell, 1996, pp.85-86.

Jacobs, Stephen. *Boris Karloff: More than a Monster*. Tomohawk Press, 2011.

Johnson, Tom, *Censored Screams: The British Ban on Hollywood Horror in the Thirties*, Jefferson: McFarland, 1997.

Johnson, Tom and del Vecchio, Deborah, *Hammer Films: An Exhaustive Filmography*, Jefferson: McFarland, 1996.

Jowett, Lorna and Stacey Abbott, *TV Horror: Investigating the Dark Side of the Small Screen*, London: I.B.Tauris, 2013.

Kendrick, James, 'A Nasty Situation: Social Panics, Transnationalism and the Video Nasty', in Steffen Hantke (ed), *Horror Film: Creating and Marketing Fear*, Jackson: University of Mississippi Press, 2004, pp.153-164.

Lee, Christopher, *Tall, Dark and Gruesome*, London: Victor Gollancz, 1997.

Leeder, Murray, 'Collective Screams: William Castle and the Gimmick Film', *Journal of Popular Culture*, vol.44, iss. 4, 2011, pp.773-795.

Leggett, Paul, *Terence Fisher: Horror, Myth and Religion*, Jefferson: McFarland, 2002.

Lowe, Victoria. '"Stages of Performance": Adaptation and Intermediality in *Theatre of Blood* (1973)', *Adaptation*, vol.3, no.2, 2010, pp.99-111.

Martin, Sara, 'In Mary Shelley's Loving Arms: Brian Aldiss's *Frankenstein Unbound* and its Film Adaptation by Roger Corman', *Foundation*, vol.89, 2003, pp.76-92.

Marwick, Arthur, *Culture in Britain since 1945*, Oxford: Basil Blackwell, 1991.

Maxford, Howard, *Hammer, House of Horror: Behind the Screams*, London: B.T. Batsford, 1996.

Macdonald, DL, *Poor Polidori*, Toronto: Toronto University Press, 1991.

McFarlane, Brian, *Novel to Film: An Introduction to the Theory of Adaptation*, Oxford: Clarendon Press, 1996.

Meikle, Denis, *A History of Horrors: The Rise and Fall of the House of Hammer*, rev.edn, Lanham, Maryland: Scarecrow Press, 2009.

Miller, Mark A, *Christopher Lee and Peter Cushing and Horror Cinema: A Filmography of their 22 Collaborations*, Jefferson: McFarland, 1995.

Monk, Claire, 'The Heritage Film and Gendered Spectatorship', *Close Up: The Electronic Journal of British Cinema* http://www.shu.ac.uk/services/lc/closeup/monk.htm

Murray, Simone, 'Materializing Adaptation Theory: The Adaptation Industry', *Literature/Film Quarterly*, vol.36, no.1, 2008, pp.4-20.

Newman, Kim (ed), *The BFI Companion to Horror*. London: Cassell, 1996.

_____, 'Jimmy Sangster obituary', *Guardian*, 22 August, 2011, http://www.theguardian.com/film/2011/aug/21/jimmy-sangster-obituary

Nicholson, Peter, interview with Terence Fisher in *Cinefastastique*, 1976, reprinted in *Cine Resort*, http://cine-resort.blogspot.com.au/2013/10/terence-fisher-underlining.html

Patterson, John, 'Peeping Tom may have been nasty but it didn't deserve critics' cold shoulder', *The Guardian*, 13 November, 2010, http://www.theguardian.com/film/2010/nov/13/peeping-tom-john-patterson

Petley, Julian, 'The Lost Continent', in Charles Barr (ed), *All Our Yesterdays: 90 Years of British Cinema*, London, British Film Institute, 1986, pp.98-119.

Petrie, Duncan, 'Innovation and Economy: The Contribution of the Gainsborough Cinematographer', in Pam Cook (ed), *Gainsborough Pictures*, London: Cassell, 1997, pp.118-136.

Pirie, David, *Hammer: A Cinema Case Study,* London: British Film Institute, 1981.

_____, *A Heritage of Horror: The English Gothic Cinema 1946-1972*, London: Gordon Fraser, 1973.

Policante, Amedeo, 'Vampires of Capital: Gothic Reflections between Horror and Hope', *Cultural Logic*, 2010.

Raggio, Olga, 'The Myth of Prometheus: its Survival and Metamorphoses up to the Eighteenth Century', *Journal of the Warburg and Courtauld Institutes*, vol.21, no.1/2, 1958, pp.44-62.

Ray, Robert B. 'The Field of "Literature and Film"', in James Naremore (ed), *Film Adaptation*, London: Athlone Press, 2000, pp.38-53.

Ross, Robert, *The Carry On Story*, London: Reynolds and Hearn, 2005.

Salisbury, Mark, 'Graveyard Shift', *Fangoria*, November 1999.

Sanders, Julie, *Adaptation and Appropriation*, London: Routledge, 2006.

Sangster, Jimmy, *Do you Want it Good or Tuesday? From Hammer Films to Hollywood: A Life in Movies*, Midnight Marquee Press, 2009.

Scott, Walter, 'Modern Prometheus: A Novel', *Blackwood's Edinburgh Magazine*, vol.2, no.20 March-1 April, 1818, pp.613-620.

Sedgwick, Eve Kosofsky, *The Coherence of Gothic Conventions*, London: Methuen, 1986.

Shelley, Mary, *Frankenstein, or, the Modern Prometheus* (ed. Maurice Hindle), Harmondsworth: Penguin, 1985 (reissued 1992).

Stam, Robert, 'Beyond Fidelity: The Dialogics of Adaptation', in James Naremore (ed), *Film Adaptation*, London: Athlone Press, 2000, pp.54-76.

_____, *Literature Through Film: Realism, Magic and the Art of Adaptation*, Oxford: Blackwell, 2005.

_____ and Raengo, Allesandra (eds), *Companion to Literature and Film*, Oxford: Blackwell, 2008.

Young, Rob, 'Daniel Radcliff gives us a new twist on a twisted character', *Cinelinx*, December 2013. www.cinelinx.com/movie-news/item/5007-daniel-radcliff-gives-us-a-new-twist-on-a-twisted-character.html

Frightmares
A History of British Horror Cinema
Ian Cooper

DEVIL'S ADVOCATES

"Auteur Publishing's new Devil's Advocates critiques on individual titles offer bracingly fresh perspectives from passionate writers. The series will perfectly complement the BFI archive volumes." Christopher Fowler, Independent on Sunday

LET THE RIGHT ONE IN — ANNE BILLSON

"Anne Billson offers an accessible, lively but thoughtful take on the '80s-set Swedish vampire belter... a fun, stimulating exploration of a modern masterpiece." Empire

WITCHFINDER GENERAL — IAN COOPER

"I enjoyed it very much; it sets out all the various influences, both before and after the film, and indeed the essence of the film itself, very well indeed." Jonathan Rigby, author of English Gothic

SAW — BENJAMIN POOLE

"This is a great addition to a series of books that are starting to become compulsory for horror fans. It will also help you to appreciate just what an original and amazing experience the original SAW truly was." The Dark Side

THE TEXAS CHAIN SAW MASSACRE — JAMES ROSE

"[James Rose] find[s] new and unusual perspectives with which to address [the] censor-baiting material. Unsurprisingly, the effect... is to send the reader back to the films... watch the films, read these Devil's Advocate analyses of them." Crime Time